New Directions for
Institutional Research

Gloria Crisp
EDITOR

Legal Considerations for Assessment and Institutional Research Leaders

Matthew B. Fuller

EDITOR

Number 172
Jossey-Bass
San Francisco

Legal Considerations for Assessment and Institutional Research Leaders
Matthew B. Fuller (ed.)
New Directions for Institutional Research, no. 172
Editor: Gloria Crisp

NEW DIRECTIONS FOR INSTITUTIONAL RESEARCH, (Print ISSN: 0271-0579; Online ISSN: 1536-075X), is published quarterly by Wile
Subscription Services, Inc., a Wiley Company, 111 River St., Hoboken, NJ 07030-5774 USA.
Postmaster: Send all address changes to *NEW DIRECTIONS FOR INSTITUTIONAL RESEARCH*, John Wiley & Sons Inc., C/O The Sherida
Press, PO Box 465, Hanover, PA 17331 USA.

Information for subscribers
NEW DIRECTIONS FOR INSTITUTIONAL RESEARCH is published in 4 issues per year. Institutional subscription prices for 2017 are:
Print & Online: US$461 (US), US$515 (Canada & Mexico), US$561 (Rest of World), €366 (Europe), £2890 (UK). Prices are excl
sive of tax. Asia-Pacific GST, Canadian GST/HST and European VAT will be applied at the appropriate rates. For more information c
current tax rates, please go to www.wileyonlinelibrary.com/tax-vat. The price includes online access to the current and all online bac
files to January 1st 2013, where available. For other pricing options, including access information and terms and conditions, please vis
www.wileyonlinelibrary.com/access.

Delivery Terms and Legal Title
Where the subscription price includes print issues and delivery is to the recipient's address, delivery terms are **Delivered at Place (DAP**
the recipient is responsible for paying any import duty or taxes. Title to all issues transfers FOB our shipping point, freight prepaid. We w
endeavour to fulfil claims for missing or damaged copies within six months of publication, within our reasonable discretion and subject
availability.

Back issues: Single issues from current and recent volumes are available at the current single issue price from cs-journals@wiley.com.

Publisher: *NEW DIRECTIONS FOR INSTITUTIONAL RESEARCH* is published by Wiley Periodicals, Inc., 350 Main St., Malden, MA 0214
5020.

Journal Customer Services: For ordering information, claims and any enquiry concerning your journal subscription please go
www.wileycustomerhelp.com/ask or contact your nearest office.
Americas: Email: cs-journals@wiley.com; Tel: +1 781 388 8598 or +1 800 835 6770 (toll free in the USA & Canada).
Europe, Middle East and Africa: Email: cs-journals@wiley.com; Tel: +44 (0) 1865 778315.
Asia Pacific: Email: cs-journals@wiley.com; Tel: +65 6511 8000.
Japan: For Japanese speaking support, Email: cs-japan@wiley.com.
Visit our Online Customer Help available in 7 languages at www.wileycustomerhelp.com/ask

Production Editor: Poornita Jugran (email: pjugran@wiley.com).

Printed in the USA by The Sheridan Group.

Address for Editorial Correspondence: Editor-in chief, John F. Ryan, *NEW DIRECTIONS FOR INSTITUTIONAL RESEARCH*, Em
jfryan@uvm.edu

Abstracting and Indexing Services
The Journal is indexed by Academic Search (EBSCO Publishing); Academic Search Alumni Edition (EBSCO Publishing); Academic Sea
Elite (EBSCO Publishing); Academic Search Premier (EBSCO Publishing); ERA: Educational Research Abstracts Online (T&F); ER
Educational Resources Information Center (CSC); Higher Education Abstracts (Claremont Graduate University); Professional Developm
Collection (EBSCO Publishing).

Cover design: Wiley
Cover Images: © Lava 4 images | Shutterstock

For submission instructions, subscription and all other information visit:
wileyonlinelibrary.com/journal/ir

THE ASSOCIATION FOR INSTITUTIONAL RESEARCH (AIR) is the world's largest professional association for institutional researchers. The organization provides educational resources, best practices, and professional development opportunities for more than 4,000 members. Its primary purpose is to support members in the process of collecting, analyzing, and converting data into information that supports decision making in higher education.

Contents

EDITOR'S NOTES

Many institutional research (IR) staff have their introduction to legal processes when a general counsel asks for data to support an institutional defense strategy. Prior volumes of *New Directions for Institutional Research* (Jones, 1997; Luna, 2008) illustrate how IR staff members' skillsets can be tremendous assets to institutional legal defenses or in averting legal action altogether. This volume takes a different approach and is aimed at helping IR staff navigate the legal morasses they might face in their unique roles as IR leaders. Despite the nearly unanimous recognition that higher education is an exceptionally litigious environment (Lake, 2013; Montgomery, 1997), no treatments of legal issues IR staff might face have been published, leaving IR staff with a dearth of guidance in responding to legal issues.

In this volume, legal counselors have partnered with IR staff, enriching each other's perspectives and offering readers examples for applying suggested practices. The monograph opens by offering the reader a framework for using legal precedents and law as a framework for guiding practice and policies, the Practices, Policies, and Legal Boundaries (PPLB) framework. The PPLB framework is flexible and IR staff can apply a variety of interpretations of the law while also clarifying legal boundaries that cannot be violated. Next, I offer an update on the Family Educational Rights and Privacy Act (FERPA). Then, Katie Beaudin offers guidance on dealing with data security breaches and partnering with third-party vendors. William Knight and Elizabeth Lugg partner to review employment, discrimination, harassment, intellectual property, and export control laws that could find their way to the IR leader's desk. Special attention was paid to offering a detailed yet readable overview of relevant law as well as examples of how these laws might apply to typical IR situations. Next, Timothy Letzring illustrates how knowledge of particular situations or impending developments—which IR staff often see developing in data—could constitute legal liability for institutions. This chapter makes a number of important recommendations about organizational leadership and cross-campus communication as means to limiting liability. Next, Julee Flood and Jeffery Roberts examine the historical development of regional accreditation and predict how courts might shift their perspectives on accreditation as a voluntary effort to one that may be treated with contractual or even constitutional protections in the future. Next, Rhonda Beassie asks whether IR data and rhetoric establish a duty to improve. In essence she helps readers grapple with legal commitments IR staff and institutional leaders might make in the normal course of their

New Directions for Institutional Research, no. 172 © 2017 Wiley Periodicals, Inc.
Published online in Wiley Online Library (wileyonlinelibrary.com) • DOI: 10.1002/ir.20199

duties. Finally, Gage Paine synthesizes all of these chapters into a reflection on the role of IR in a litigious environment, offering sound leadership advice for IR staff.

In addition to drawing from existing case law, the authors' expertise also informs other noteworthy areas of legal consideration for IR staff. For example, faculty plaintiffs have made a number of nuanced arguments about course and faculty evaluations (see *Clark v. Whiting* (1979); *Earl v. Norfolk* (2014); or *Siu v. Johnson* (1984)). As many IR offices oversee the collection and dissemination of course evaluations, familiarity with legal issues surrounding faculty and course evaluation systems might prove beneficial. This need is fully addressed in prior literature (see Kaplin & Lee, 2014, pp. 231–253). For this reason (and since courts have generally adopted a pattern of nonintrusion on academic quality issues), legal issues surrounding faculty and course evaluations are not addressed in this monograph.

Throughout the volume, every attempt has been made to offer examples of how legal precedents may be applied to typical IR situations. Common threads throughout many chapters is that IR staff face little in terms of legal liabilities that are unique to their roles and that the jurisprudence on IR practice is evolving. The treatment of legal issues in IR practice could not be completely addressed in the span of one short monograph. With this in mind, we view this monograph as the beginning of future discourse and developments in an area of important concern for IR staff.

Matthew Fuller
Editor

References

Clark v. Whiting, 607 F.2d 634 (4th Cir. 1979).
Earl v. Norfolk State University, WL 6608769 (2014).
Jones, L. G. (Ed.). (1997). *Preventing lawsuits: The role of institutional research. New Directions for Institutional Research, 96*(Winter). San Francisco, CA: Jossey-Bass.
Kaplin, W. A., & Lee, B. A. (2014). *The law of higher education.* San Francisco, CA: Jossey-Bass.
Lake, P. F. (2013, July/August). Welcome to Compliance U: The board's role in the regulatory era. *Trusteeship, 21*(4), Article 1. Retrieved from http://agb.org/trusteeship/2013/7/welcome-compliance-u-boards-role-regulatory-era
Luna, A. L. (2008). Editor's notes. In A. L. Luna, *Legal applications of data for institutional research* (pp. 1–4). San Francisco, CA: Jossey-Bass.
Montgomery, J. R. (1997). This legal stuff is getting serious. In L. G. Jones (Ed.), *Preventing lawsuits: The role of institutional research. New Directions for Institutional Research, 96* (pp. 7–18). San Francisco, CA: Jossey-Bass.
Siu v. Johnson, 748 F.2d 238 (4th Cir. 1984).

Matthew Fuller, *PhD, Associate Professor, Higher Education Leadership, Sam Houston State University.*

1

After examining typical legal contexts for IR practice, this chapter offers the Practices, Policies, and Legal Boundaries (PPLB) framework for using laws as guidelines for policy and practice.

The Practices, Policies, and Legal Boundaries Framework in Assessment and Institutional Research

Matthew Fuller, PhD

If given enough years, institutional research (IR) leaders will likely hear the dreaded "L" word: Lawsuit! Few words direct so much institutional action so quickly, broadly, and decisively as this one. And that is with good reason. The costs for settling claims from higher education lawsuits are astronomical. The University of Central Florida (Russon, 2016), the Maricopa County Community College District (Faller, 2014), Rockhurst University (Robertson, 2016), the University of Miami (Conti, 2014), the University of California–Los Angeles (Terhune, 2015), and American University have all been in the news for lawsuits related to breaches of data security. In 2015 alone, 550 colleges or universities reported being the targets of data security breach attempts (Symantec, 2015). Often, these data breaches affect thousands of students and result in years of expensive litigation and reputational harm for institutions (O'Neil, 2014). Some litigation, such as UCLA's, end favorably for the university, with the institution avoiding 1.25 million dollars in damages paid to plaintiffs (Terhune, 2015). However, not all cases end favorably for the institution. For instance, a case with Maricopa County Community College recently resulted in the university paying $2,500 for each affected individual, totaling $2.5 million in damages (Pham, 2014). Regardless of the outcome, all of the above-mentioned cases had considerable costs to the institution including lawyer's fees, repairs, insurance premiums, lost time, and damage to institutional reputation.

Traditionally, IR staff have been called to support institutions looking to argue a defense strategy using sound institutional data (Montgomery, 1997). This is fortunate as there are relatively few instances in which IR staff are directly named as litigants in a suit. However, for anyone facing a lawsuit, this is of little solace. The first chapter of this volume briefly examines the typical arguments under which IR staff face legal action and

NEW DIRECTIONS FOR INSTITUTIONAL RESEARCH, no. 172 © 2017 Wiley Periodicals, Inc.
Published online in Wiley Online Library (wileyonlinelibrary.com) • DOI: 10.1002/ir.20200

outlines a framework—the Practices, Policies, and Legal Boundaries (PPLB) framework—guiding how IR leaders can use legal precedents and laws as guide for effective, legallyprudent IR practice. Before addressing the elements of the PPLB framework, I review the ways in which IR colleagues have faced litigation.

Overview of Prior IR Litigation

Cases involving IR staff members as direct litigants have traditionally drawn upon three forms of law: (1) employment and discrimination laws, (2) whistleblower laws, and (3) laws or tort actions pertaining to data breaches or security. In reviewing the WestLaw database, over 80 cases brought by or directly involving IR staff have been argued in federal and state cases since 1970. Despite the unique role of institutional research in academe, there is very little that distinguishes IR professionals as different from other offices on campus in regards to the law. This presents an opportunity for IR professionals to learn from situations that extend beyond institutional research such as employment, discrimination, and harassment issues, which are often managed by human resources or legal counsel staff.

Employment and Discrimination Laws.   First, over half of the legal cases involving IR staff since 1970 have dealt with the termination of an IR staff member and are argued under the aegis of employment law. Most cases involving IR staff have been argued on the grounds of some form of discrimination. For example, in *Mitchell v. University of Louisiana System* (2015) the plaintiff, Melinda Mitchell, claimed that she was passed over for a promotion when a younger, White staff member was hired for an advanced IR position. Arguing discrimination on the grounds of age, race, and gender, Mitchell's claims were not supported by the court since Mitchell lacked a graduate degree and "no reasonable juror would find racial or sexual discrimination" (*Mitchell v. Univ. of Louisiana Sys.*, 2015). Such findings, wherein a court favors the university's autonomy in making its own employment and academic decisions, are typical of most IR employment and discrimination cases (Montgomery, 1997). Similarly, in *Thomas v. Kirkwood Community College* (1971), a plaintiff's due process claim was unsuccessfully raised in seeking to enjoin the college from terminating her employment. In short, institutions were granted considerable latitude in making employment and academic decisions, though decisions must afford employees, staff, and student basic due process, nondiscrimination, and nonharassment protections (see Chapter 4 of this volume).

Whistleblower Laws.   Approximately a tenth of the cases involving IR professionals have been argued on the grounds of retaliatory termination or whistleblower protections. In some cases arguments have included retaliation against IR staff for levying discrimination claims (e.g., *Schbley v. Gould, Wije v. University of Texas Medical Branch at Galveston*). IR professionals may become aware of inefficient operations, financial mistakes, or ethics violations by viewing data in the normal course of their duties. If their efforts to correct these concerns are met with retaliatory, adverse employment actions, the IR staff member could substantiate a legal case under various state whistleblower laws. For example, in *Walstrom v. State of Oklahoma* (2009), the plaintiff, Jana Walstrom, was an IR staff member who, through the normal course of her duties, discovered that funds for a therapeutic horse-riding program were being misappropriated to other programs. Two days after emailing and calling her supervisors and other senior leaders, Walstrom was terminated. In crafting her legal argument, Walstrom's attorney relied on Oklahoma's Whistleblower Act and yet failed to demonstrate that considerations of the allocation of funding were matters explicitly afforded Walstrom in her job duties. As such, Walstrom's speech and actions in pointing out irregularities in funding were not formally recognized in her written job responsibilities and therefore could be subject to employer discipline as a form of insubordination or lack of focus on required duties.

Actions Involving Breaches of Data Security.   Third, a small but growing number of legal actions involving IR staff have focused on breaches of data security. Although many institutions are accustomed to data confidentiality measures and acts, risks related to data breaches are a growing area of concern as hacking and phishing attacks grow in sophistication, scope, and complexity (O'Neil, 2014). As such, cases resulting from data security breaches are increasing in frequency, reputational risk, and financial loss (O'Neil, 2014). Some of these cases have involved criminal litigation against staff members alleged to have intentionally violated data security measures.

A small number of instances wherein IR professionals have used data access authorizations illegally or falsified data have also been noted. Most of these situations are dealt with internally and have settled out of court, thereby limiting the ability to provide a citation or legal brief for others to review. IR professionals may find it useful to refer to other functional areas of the university that have faced stringent litigation under the False Claims Act (31 USC §§ 3729–3733). For example, in *Kreipke v. Wayne State University* (2015), an assistant professor claimed that he was retaliatorily dismissed for raising a claim that Wayne State University had artificially inflated the data regarding federal grant funding. The Sixth Circuit Court of Appeals found that the university was an "arm of the state," and not a "person," (line 7) as defined under the False Claims Act and therefore enjoyed a particular level of sovereign immunity. The case commanded considerable time and institutional resources (Fischler, 2015). Moreover, as Chemerinsky (2001) noted, winning legal cases on the grounds of sovereign immunity seldom does much good for an institution's image in the eyes of the public.

The Balancing Act of IR

As Volkwein (1999) noted, IR leaders' unique roles place them front and center of tensions inherent in modern academe. Perhaps more than any other skill, negotiating tricky, complex situations—engaging in the *balancing act of IR*—is a necessary to the success of IR professionals. By "balancing act," I suggest that negotiation skills are critical to the everyday work of all higher education leaders, but particularly IR leaders. Being able to maintain faculty participation in institutional decision-making processes while also explaining to faculty members that the institution will be subject to an ever-increasing body of legislative acts takes grace, tact, and *balancing skills*. Being able to listen actively to both sides of an alleged harassment situation and show both sides genuine concern while also directly and decisively dealing with confirmed misconduct takes courage and *balancing skills*. Providing for the data access needs of faculty, researchers, and staff while also coping with pressures on the institution to maintain secure data stores requires *balancing skills*. Indeed, balancing the needs of internal or local constituents with the needs of external governing agencies, political action agencies, or members of the public at large is a persistent challenge for IR leaders.

Here, legal guidance—in the form of judicial case opinions or findings, interpretations of federal or state legislation, or professional organization resources—can inform leadership practices in making legally prudent decisions. Guidance from professional organizations such as the Association for Institutional Research (AIR), the Education Law Association, the Higher Education Compliance Alliance (2015), and other professional organizations can help IR leaders stay abreast of legal issues and cases. Moreover, a growing number of IR graduate preparation programs include course content specific to legal concepts, though this topic is seldom taught outside of doctoral-level programs. Despite the growing number of resources and information available regarding legal issues in higher education, information is typically not written for an IR audience or does not specifically address legal issues faced by IR practitioners. Therefore, IR leaders may be left searching for guidance on how to respond to legal situations. In response, I offer readers the following framework for reflecting on how their practice fits within the boundaries of currently accepted legal precedents.

Practices, Policies, and Legal Boundaries Framework

The Practices, Policies, and Legal Boundaries (PPLB) framework is a framework for administrative leadership to consider how laws can inform IR policies and practices. I have used the PPLB framework for a number of years in IR leadership roles and have found it useful in IR practice. Though the examples of its application in this chapter are focused on IR, leaders from other areas of the university may find use in the framework. I begin by

**Figure 1.1. The Legal Boundaries Framework for Policy
and Practice—Full Alignment**

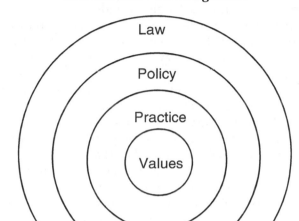

outlining the central tenets of the PPLB framework before discussing patent
applications of the framework to IR scenarios.

Central Tenets of the PPLB Framework. The PPLB framework
is built around institutional values and thus offers a natural point of
common support for faculty, staff, administrators, and students. The PPLB
framework may be considered an ecological framework as it includes
institutional values reflected in Bronfenbrenner's (1979) exosystem and
also spans the microsystem. The PPLB framework is, however, far more
nuanced than a simple recognition of institutional values. As an ecological
framework, it relies on three interrelated layers: practice, policy, and law.
Each layer is bounded by an outer layer offering the widest feasible interpretation within which an inner layer may operate (see Figure 1.1). It is
therefore critical to view each outer layer not as an impermeable boundary
but as a flexible guideline open, in some instances, to considerable interpretation, and in others, to strict interpretation. Explained differently, each
outer layer is the widest possible realm of operation for the inner layers that
have varying amount of flexibility or context-dependent interpretations.

The innermost layer, the institutional values layer, colors the ways in
which practice and policy are implemented at an institution. Next, the practice layer surrounds institutional values and concerns itself with how faculty, staff, and administrators engage in their daily operations and how they
conduct themselves in the course of completing their job responsibilities.
Practice is typified by the actions institutional constituents engage in as they

seek to achieve institutional goals. The first two layers of the PPLB framework are bounded by a third layer: the policy layer. In the PPLB framework policy is taken to mean formalized, written guidelines meant to inform practice. Thus, in the PPLB framework, policy is assumed to provide the outermost boundary within which effective, legitimate practice can and should occur. Stated differently, the policy layer paints the boundaries within which practices can be considered permissible and in accord with institutional values. For example, data collection or retention practices are not only a function of institutional values but also stated policies.

Drawing a distinction between policies as formal written statements and practices as actions is critical in reflecting dichotomies in espoused and real values. In crafting a definition of policy that is a formal, written statement, I considered how IR staff engage in a given pattern even though few written standards (policies) are available. IR leaders in this case operate through their understanding of practice, rather than policy. Many institutional staff have grappled with how to conduct business (practice) when few written policies exist. One central concept of the PPLB framework is the notion that if written policy does not exist, the more basal layer of practice will inherently fill that gap. The process wherein policy gaps are filled by practice is highly individualized, personal, and influenced by politics, organizational culture, leadership styles and dynamics, and institutional values. The difficulty that such a lack of written policy places on institutional constituents is easy to understand. Such a situation requires professionals to "ad lib" or "make it up as they go" which is neither an ideal position for the individual nor an advisable condition for institutional liability.

For example, when James Meredith attempted to enroll in classes at the predominately White University of Mississippi (also referred to as Ole Miss) in 1961, a long legal and political battle ensued. The institution's legal defense strategy rested on the argument that there was no formal policy of segregation at Ole Miss and instead questioned Meredith's transfer of hours and other anomalies that were supported via Mississippi state statues (Donovan, 2002). During the court proceedings, Meredith's defense team had to prove that the segregation—which was prevalent at Ole Miss—had become practice since no formal policy statement regarding segregation existed.

Though dated, the Meredith case may serve as an example of how the outermost law layer of the PPLB can shape how policies and practices may be considered legally permissible. Legal guidance, in the form of case law, judicial opinion, or governmental or legislative acts, should serve as a guide for what may be considered legally permissible. Yet, law should also be interpreted in such a way that professionals feel comfortable responding to the various issues facing higher education institutions. For this reason, the law layer is the broadest and the most open to interpretation as it represents the widest boundary in the PPLB framework.

NEW DIRECTIONS FOR INSTITUTIONAL RESEARCH • DOI: 10.1002/ir

Additional Considerations.   The boundaries between each layer of the PPLB framework should be important areas of consideration for IR professionals. Within each boundary there are a number of colleagues who can aid in understanding the different characteristics of each layer. For example, legal counsel, various senior administrators, or faculty members can be excellent resources in staying abreast of new laws and legal developments. Human resources staff and administrators in a number of offices likely possess a strong grasp of institutional policies, and faculty and staff engaging in daily practices should be consulted when changes in policy/practice are anticipated.

Although not a formal layer of the PPLB, ethics also play a vital role in how individuals interpret law and policy and influence how individuals engage in practices. It is critical to recognize the assumption that professionals hoping to engage in legally permissible practices will also be operating ethically and vice versa. It is expected that including an ethical layer in the framework may complicate rather than provide clarity to issues. It is recommended, however, that IR leaders draw from professional guidance codified in the Association for Institutional Research's Code of Ethics (2013) as ethical behavior in most cases coincides with legally permissible practice.

Benefits and Applications of the PPLB Framework.   The layered nature of the PPLB framework affords various possibilities for IR and other higher education professionals to consider how legal precedents serve to influence policy and practice. First, it offers opportunities to visualize instances in which practice extends or rests outside of policy without breaching a legal foundation (Figure 1.2) or in which practice extends both policy and legal guidance (Figure 1.3). Second, professionals may also consider how policy alone can be found to be in violation of a legal perspective (Figure 1.4). Each of these scenarios offers unique challenges to higher education leaders. By visualizing these breaches, institutional leaders may be able to develop appropriate responses to bring policies or practices in line with legal guidance, thereby bringing about conditions in which the university is most likely to succeed in achieving its vision. As such, using the PPLB framework as a reflective framework for aligning practice, policy, and legal boundaries may also aid in avoiding lengthy and costly legal battles.

PPLB Framework in Full Alignment.   As shown in Figure 1.1, when the PPLB framework is in full alignment, practices are conducted within the boundaries of policies, which are within the boundaries of applicable laws, and all layers are guided by institutional values. Offices, faculty, and staff, and administrators are all operating in an efficient manner, having minimized the likelihood they are operating "outside of the law" or "against policy." When operating in full alignment, pressures warranting immediate action are minimized and IR leaders can reflect upon ways in which law and policy might augment or inform practice. The PPLB framework is fluid and flexible, representing practice and policy interactions as either closely crafted in reference to an outer layer or not. Though still in full alignment,

Figure 1.2. Policy or Practice Just Within Bounds

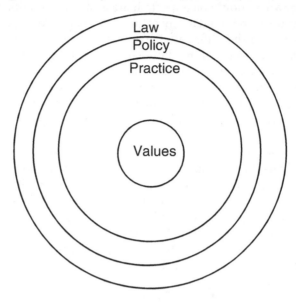

Figure 1.3. Practice Breaching Policy

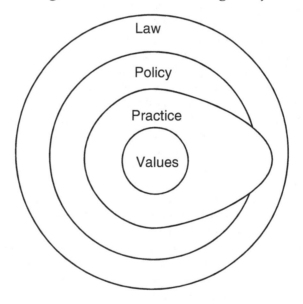

IR professionals can use the PPLB framework to visualize how their practice or policies may be so closely aligned to legal boundaries that they may be placing highly autonomous staff in situations where they face near occasions to misinterpret policy, act outside of policy or law, or where they

Figure 1.4. Practice Breaching Policy and Law

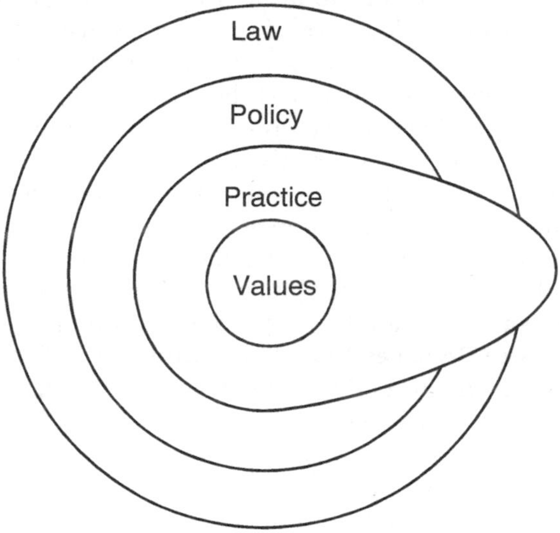

have room to develop innovative practices. It is important to note that policies can be closely tailored to match legal guidance and practices can be closely tailored to policies. For example, many IR offices derive data access policies from the Family Educational Rights and Privacy Act (FERPA) and these policies, in turn, are crafted so as to limit wide interpretations and practices, as depicted in Figure 1.2. Given the high stakes involved in violating confidentiality of students' educational records, crafting policies, and implementing practices that closely reflect FERPA guidelines is a reasonable institutional response.

When Practice Breaches Policy.   While it is important to remember the individuals behind the policy, we must also remember that policies, by nature, codify a set of practices that ensure organizational, rather than individual stability. For instance, faculty or staff members operating outside of the policy may be operating in what they see as the best course of action, but may also be doing so with a limited set of information about how their practice affects organizational constituents or from a biased frame of reference. Acting outside the policy may place such professionals in a difficult legal situation wherein they consciously choose not to follow a policy that was correctly or incorrectly believed to be flawed or wherein their actions are not condoned by the institution (see Figure 1.3).

IR professionals often act as "street level bureaucrats" (Lipsky, 1969) or leaders making context-dependent judgments about how to apply policies. For example, IR staff face tremendous numbers of requests for data every day. At the same time, policies may also require requests for institutional data to be formally made to an IR director. This policy ensures that the director can efficiently manage incoming requests and can confirm that such requests are legitimate and fall within the scope of IR work. Usually the director will delegate the work to an analyst or data manager with guidelines to provide high levels of customer support. However, customers may circumvent office policy by going around the director and making a request directly to the analyst. The analyst who is under pressure to provide high levels of customer support may directly respond to the request without approval from the director, thereby engaging in a practice that breaches office policy. Though seemingly innocuous, such behavior could contribute to legal action wherein a plaintiff's counsel could depict the IR office as poorly managed. It is therefore critical that practice breaches of policy be addressed in the internal workings of an IR office and/or institution.

When Practice Breaches Both Policy and Law.   Some of the most challenging legal scenarios derive from instances in which an employee's actions violated both stated policy and law (see Figure 1.4). In many ways, these situations can be easy to interpret. Nonetheless, these scenarios are not always easy to address and can unfortunately be many IR professionals' first introduction to institutional legal counsel. Practice breaches of policy and law are especially problematic from an institutional liability perspective because policies that were well-reasoned enough to be established within the boundaries of legal guidance were broken. In such conditions, the entire panoply of remedies and institutional protections could be considered depending on the severity of the violation.

The commonly faced scenario of sharing or withholding student data may be illustrative here. Most institutions possess policies articulating how institutional staff are to share data and many IR offices maintain tracking systems detailing the kinds of requests being made, "customers" being served, and the length of time to complete requests for data. Moreover, institutions may also have statements or policies indicating that they do not discriminate against individuals on a basis of race, gender, ethnicity, and so forth. As a part of the institution's student organization recognition process, a student group may be required by policy to demonstrate a need for their group's existence and may be required to consult the IR office to obtain data on student demographics or student performance metrics that would be served by the group. Suppose the IR staff member, operating under an abundance of care, refuses to provide these data to one particular student group, effectively ensuring the group will not be recognized. However, months later the staff member provides a similar report to another group of students representing a different ethnic group, thereby facilitating their recognition. Such actions might be fodder for a discrimination lawsuit by violating both policy and discrimination law.

When Policy Breaches Law.   When policy breaches law, practice falls within the boundaries of legal guidance while policy guidelines breach legal guidance (see Figure 1.5). In this instance, formal, written policies are found to be outside the boundaries of acceptable legal precedent and yet

NEW DIRECTIONS FOR INSTITUTIONAL RESEARCH • DOI: 10.1002/ir

Figure 1.5. Policy Breaching Law

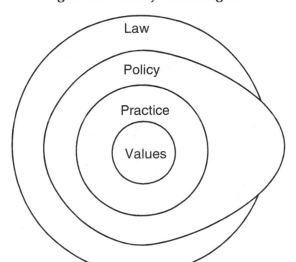

practices are within the boundaries of law. Often, flaws in policy go un-noticed until a practice shines light on an inefficiency. However, through careful reflection, IR staff can identify areas wherein policies are illegal long before practices are found to be illegal. This work takes time, reflection, and innovation to develop new policies and influence future practice. Moreover, new policies require training and further evaluation to determine whether policy enhancements are having intended or unintended effects. Nonethe-less, the fact that faculty and staff are operating within legal boundaries—despite policy inefficiencies—affords opportunities to correct policy posi-tions prior to legal action. Therefore, policy analysis, revisions, and training can bring policies back within legal boundaries. Still, special interest groups and student activists could become aware of illegal policies and could press for legal action even if practices were not noted, though their arguments could be significantly bolstered if practices also breached policy and legal boundaries.

When Practice and Policy Breach Law.   IR staff can operate well within the boundaries of an established institutional policy, but their practice and policy may both be outside of the boundaries of law. Such conditions represent a complex challenge for institutional leaders and general counsel. Learning that one's actions are at once compliant with institutional policy and illegal can be disillusioning. In this instance, new policies and subsequent training may be in order, yet respectful advocacy to refine legal parameters might also be considered. These situations offer IR leaders opportunities to scan their organizations, engage in dialogue with

Figure 1.6. Policy and Practice Breaching Law

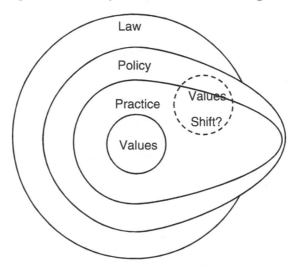

others within and outside of the organization, and develop a plan for refined practice.

The idea that practice and policy align but remain outside of law may also signal a value shift that can be critically important for institutional communities to recognize (see Figure 1.6). Understanding how faculty and staff enact policies can give IR leaders clues to how faculty and staff see themselves fitting into the institutional value system. IR leaders may seek to establish polices and later, practices, that are consonant with law or may seek to refine law through normal routes of advocacy. Seeing how faculty and staff engage in their daily practices and how they interpret and apply policies can be vital to charting a stable future for institutions amid legal shifts. One such example might be institutions that adopted antidiscrimination policies and practices for same-sex couples long before the U.S. Supreme Court decision *Obergefell v. Hodges* (2015). As noted in the Supreme Court's opinion, "As more than 100 amici make clear in their filings, many of the central institutions in American life—state and local governments, the military, large and small businesses, labor unions, religious organizations, law enforcement, civic groups, professional organizations, and universities—have devoted substantial attention to the question [of gay marriage] (p. 24)." College and university activism played a role in bringing law up to date with higher education practice and policy.

In contrast, many religiously affiliated institutions that did not have nondiscrimination policies or practices in place for same-sex couples or had policies or practices that countered the new legal paradigm had to implement policies and begin training for practices. Occasionally, significant legal shifts occur, eroding a foundation for institutional practices, policies,

NEW DIRECTIONS FOR INSTITUTIONAL RESEARCH • DOI: 10.1002/ir

Figure 1.7. Legal Shift—Policy, Practice, or Values Not Supported

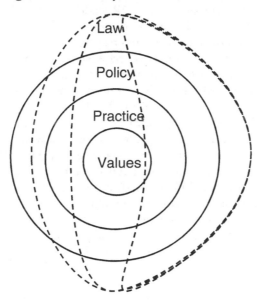

or values and necessitating institutional action (see Figure 1.7). Such legal shifts are difficult to predict yet are simultaneously often the result of lengthy, dramatic legal processes spanning years or decades. Consider, for example, the length of time it has taken affirmative action, gender identity, or sexual orientation discrimination cases to find their way through the U.S. legal system. Such developments challenge institutional response systems and require additional training, policy revision, and effective leadership to once again achieve alignment across all levels of the PPLB framework.

Conclusions

The art of IR practice and leadership requires the understanding that answers and subsequent courses of action are seldom simple, straightforward endeavors. Determining how best to respond to a challenging situation may be hampered by many factors such as a lack of information, shifting or developing contexts, swiftness with which responses are needed, and a lack of clarity about the challenges faced. Many of these situations can be directly addressed by the PPLB framework by allowing IR leaders the opportunity to visualize, plan for, and implement appropriate courses of action. Recognizing instances wherein practices and/or policies may conflict with legal precedents can be helpful in suggesting courses of action IR professionals can take to resolve conflicts or avoid potential litigation.

Although institutional research is not typically subjected to legal scrutiny, IR professionals may often face legal challenges. IR leaders must have knowledge of and work to uphold institutional employment, discrimination, finance, and harassment laws. IR leaders are also held to contractual obligations to respond to and work with vendors, service providers, faculty, and staff. Moreover, institutional research offices must address state and federal mandates for accountability requests and provide accurate data. Though IR staff have not historically been the focus of lawsuits, their unique roles as data managers, collectors, sharers, users, and reporters place IR professionals in situations that may result in legal challenges.

It is hoped that the PPLB framework and subsequent chapters in this volume will provide guidance to IR professionals in how to act appropriately within boundaries of permissible law or stated policy. The PPLB framework also offers IR leaders a new means of reflecting on and refining practices and policies to prepare for shifts in institutional values or law. In so doing, it is expected that IR leaders will be able to avoid expensive, damaging legal action. Reflecting on which elements—values, practice, and/or policy—are guided by prudent interpretations of legal precedents and governmental mandates can support effective, sustainable IR practice in some of higher education's most litigious times.

References

Association for Institutional Research. (2013). *Code of ethics and professional practice*. Tallahassee, FL: Association for Institutional Research. Retrieved from https://www.airweb.org/Membership/Pages/CodeOfEthics.aspx

Bronfenbrenner, U. (1979). *The ecology of human development: Experiments by nature and design*. Cambridge, MA: Harvard University Press.

Chemerinsky, E. (2001). Against sovereign immunity. *Stanford Law Review*, 1201–1224.

Conti, A. (2014, February 7). University of Miami Health System loses records including social security numbers. *Miami New Times*. Retrieved from http://www.miaminewtimes.com/news/university-of-miami-health-system-loses-records-including-social-security-numbers-6555529

Donovan, K. A. (2002). James Meredith and the integration of Ole Miss. *Chrestomathy*, *1*(1), 21–43.

Faller, M. B. (2014, December 17). Maricopa County colleges computer hack cost tops $26M. *The Arizona Republic*. Retrieved from http://www.azcentral.com/story/news/local/phoenix/2014/12/17/costs-repair-massive-mcccd-computer-hack-top-million/20539491/

Fischler, J. (2015, December 4). State university not subject to FCA liability, 6th Circ. finds. *Law, 360*. Retrieved from http://www.law360.com/articles/734450/state-university-not-subject-to-fca-liability-6th-circ-finds

Higher Education Compliance Alliance. (2015, December). *Higher Education Compliance Alliance Matrix*. Retrieved from Compliance Matrix: http://www.higheredcompliance.org/matrix/

Kreipke v. Wayne State University. (2015). WL 7787935.

Lipsky, M. (1969). Toward a theory of street-level bureaucracy. *IRP Discussion Papers*, *45*(1), 45–69.

Montgomery, J. R. (1997). This legal stuff is getting serious. In L. G. Jones (Ed.), *Preventing lawsuits: The role of Institutional Research* (pp. 7–18). San Francisco, CA: Jossey-Bass.

O'Neil, M. (2014, March 17). Data breaches put a dent in colleges' finances as well as reputations. *The Chronicle of Higher Education*. Retrieved from http://www.chronicle.com/article/Data-Breaches-Put-a-Dent-in/145341/

Pham, T. (2014, December 4). The cost of a data breach in 2014: An industry by industry breakdown. *Infosec Island*. Retrieved from http://www.infosecisland. com/blogview/24119-The-Cost-of-a-Data-Breach-in-2014-An-Industry-by-Industry-Breakdown-.html

Robertson, J. (2016, May 23). Rockhurst University is sued over data breach in phishing scam. *Kansas City Star*. Retrieved from http://www.kansascity. com/news/local/article79288922.html

Russon, G. (2016, February 26). UCF sued a 2nd time over data breach. *Orlando Sentinel*. Retrieved from http://www.orlandosentinel.com/features/education/ os-ucf-second-lawsuit-hack-20160226-story.html

Schbley v. Gray. (1994). 1994 WL 675045.

Symantec, Inc. (2015). *Internet security threat report*. New York, NY: Symantec, Inc. Retrieved from https://www.symantec.com/content/en/us/enterprise/other_resources/ 21347933_GA_RPT-internet-security-threat-report-volume-20-2015.pdf

Terhune, C. (2015, July 17). UCLA Health System data breach affects 4.5 million patients. *LA Times*. Retrieved from http://www.latimes.com/ business/la-fi-ucla-medical-data-20150717-story.html

Volkwein, J. F. (1999). The four faces of institutional research. *New Directions in Institutional Research*, *104*, 9–19. doi:10.1002/ir.10.

Wije v. University of Texas Medical Branch at Galveston. (2007). 2007 WL 2427981

MATTHEW FULLER, PhD, Associate Professor, Higher Education Leadership, Sam Houston State University.

2

Despite its prominence, the Family Educational Rights and Privacy Act (FERPA) is often misinterpreted and misapplied. This chapter clarifies historical developments, common misconceptions, and modern applications of the law.

An Update on the Family Educational Rights and Privacy Act

Matthew Fuller, PhD

More than any other piece of legislation, the Family Educational Rights and Privacy Act (FERPA) is recognized throughout higher education as the primary piece of legislation guiding institutional research (IR) practice. The centrality FERPA has taken in higher education has also instilled a somewhat dogmatic yet unquestioned adherence to its policies. Many faculty and staff call upon FERPA to justify actions, yet simultaneously acknowledge a lack of understanding of FERPA's fundamental concepts (MacDonald, 2008). FERPA is only one of hundreds of federal legislative acts governing higher education. The Higher Education Compliance Alliance Matrix (2015) lists 262 federal statutes influencing higher education governance and operations, including FERPA, the Health Insurance Portability and Accountability Act (HIPAA), the Freedom of Information Act (FOIA), and the Jeanne Cleary Disclosure of Campus Security Policy and Campus Crime Statistics Act (Cleary Act). Understanding and appropriately applying FERPA is a challenging task for many institutions (MacDonald, 2008) and IR professionals often serve as key institutional leaders in interpreting and applying federal and state statutes.

Misunderstanding and misapplication of FERPA's tenets can cause considerable turmoil for colleges and universities. In a recent Association for Institutional Research (AIR) survey, nearly half of IR directors indicated that an understanding FERPA is critical to their work. However, only 30% of directors had received training specific to FERPA. Over half of participants indicated that they were self-taught or that they learned about FERPA from online resources (Association for Institutional Research, 2012). As such, the complexities, nuances, and value of FERPA warrants a more thorough treatment of the acts governing student data confidentiality. This chapter covers fundamental aspects of FERPA and addresses several recent updates to the law.

NEW DIRECTIONS FOR INSTITUTIONAL RESEARCH, no. 172 © 2017 Wiley Periodicals, Inc.
Published online in Wiley Online Library (wileyonlinelibrary.com) • DOI: 10.1002/ir.20201

Historical Overview of FERPA

The Family Educational Rights and Privacy Act (20 U.S.C. § 1232g; 34 CFR Part 99; § 513 of P.L. 93–380, The Education Amendments of 1974) is a federal statute protecting students' rights to privacy of educational records. FERPA, also known as the Buckley Amendment after its principal sponsor Senator James Buckley, was signed into existence by President Ford on August 21, 1974. FERPA was enacted as an amendment to the General Education Provisions Act (GEPA) called "Protection of the Rights and Privacy of Parents and Students," and codified at 20 U.S.C. § 1232g.

FERPA has had a mixed history of formal congressional affirmation and less formal clarifications in the form of administrative memos. Being an amendment, the Act was not considered by a Senate or House subcommittee and those affected by FERPA were given no opportunity to be heard on its parameters, making FERPA a somewhat controversial act at the time of its passing. In a speech given to the Legislative Conference of Parents and Teachers shortly after FERPA was passed, Senator Buckley indicated that the Act was a necessary response to "the growing evidence of the abuse of student records across the nation" (U.S. Congress, 1975, p. 974). In the decades prior to FERPA, institutions freely shared student data and could include information about students in their files without students' knowledge.

In the 1960s and 1970s, student data were not nearly as portable as they are today. Most institutions maintained nonelectronic records on students and records were limited to paper files well into the 1990s, if not later. Student data were stored on a mainframe computer in a single room managed by just a few campus personnel. The concept of "hacking" an institution's database would have been a foreign concept to the FERPA's original policymakers. Still, Senator Buckley's speeches document the growing sentiment of concern over students' control of their own educational records.

For this reason, FERPA has undergone 11 formal, Congressional revisions and the Federal Register contains over 170 interpretations or rule revisions made by the U.S. Department of Education in the past 10 years. These revisions keep the law current with regard to new technologies, security and safety on college campuses, and new threats of cybersecurity. It is notable that today's IR leaders are the first in a generation of professionals that must deal with new forms of data (such as big data, social media data, or tracked presence or mobility data), massive stores of electronic files that can be shared or breached, and new technologies that push data out to external users. Calls for comprehensive overhauls of FERPA continue with the latest beginning in August of 2015 (Electronic Privacy Information Center, 2016). Balancing the security of student data with its use in providing effective, safe educational environments is the pressing issue defining modern IR practice. Many of the student data problems faced today did not exist just a decade ago. Moreover, the overwhelming number of revisions and interpretations make FERPA seem like somewhat of a "moving target" for many higher education professionals. Therefore, a basic understanding of FERPA's fundamental precepts is needed to allow practitioners to focus on core practices in securing student data.

Current Provisions of FERPA

FERPA's purpose is to provide parameters around conditions under which institutions may share student data. In its most basic sense, FERPA is a federal statute aimed at ensuring that institutions obtain a student's prior written consent to share a personally identifiable educational record prior to the disclosure of that record. There is a misconception that FERPA shields institutions from sharing student information altogether. Disclosure is allowed and in some instances even required. FERPA simply requires institutions to obtain a student's written consent prior to divulging their educational records. As with all legal acts, definitions matter and FERPA operationalizes a number of important definitions. For a detailed definition of terms (eligible students, personally identifiable information, educational records, directory information, disclosure), see Table 2.1 and U.S. Department of Education (2017).

FERPA permits an institution to disclose Personally Identifiable Information (PII) without prior written consent if the disclosure falls under one of several exceptions. In these instances, institutions must "give public notice of the categories of information which it has designated as [information covered under these exceptions] . . . and shall allow a reasonable period of time after such notice has been given for a parent to inform the institution or agency that any or all of the information designated should not be released without the parent's prior consent" 34 CFR 9 Sect. A § 99.3, sect. 5G. These exceptions include 11 scenarios wherein an institution may disclose data without prior written consent from a student.

First, as previously mentioned, directory information does not require prior written consent from a student in order to be disclosed. Institutional colleagues with a *legitimate education interest* also enjoy an exception to the written consent exception. FERPA does not define what constitutes a legitimate educational interest. Instead, institutions should specify criteria for determining what constitutes a legitimate educational interest and who might have such an interest in PII. A written consent exception is also offered for officials at other institutions to which a student intends to transfer. Students must be given access to these transferred files from both institutions and transfer of files may be conducted without prior written consent from students.

A number of written consent exceptions are in place to ensure easy communication with law agencies and governmental authorities. For example, specific exceptions are in place for authorized representatives of the U.S. Comptroller General, the Secretary of Education, the U.S. Department

Table 2.1. Important Definitions in FERPA

Term	Definition	Comments	Statute
Eligible Students	Students who have reached 18 years of age or are attending an institution of postsecondary education (regardless of age).	Once a student turns 18 or enters an institution of postsecondary education, FERPA rights devolve from parents to eligible students.	34 CFR 9 Sect. A § 99.3, sect. 6
Personally Identifiable Information (PII)	Information that, alone or in combination, is linked or linkable to a specific student that would allow a reasonable person in the school community, who does not have personal knowledge of the relevant circumstances, to identify the student with reasonable certainty.	PII includes any data elements or combination of elements that would make a student's identity known outside of an educational context. Examples of PII may include a student's name, address, parental information, student identification numbers, or Social Security numbers.	34 CFR 9 Sect. A § 99.3, sect. 7
Educational Records	Records that are (a) directly related to a student, and (b) maintained by a college, university, or an agency working on behalf of the college or university.	Educational records do not include records or notes maintained by the creator of such a record if it is not shared with anyone else or is created to be a personal memory aid or note.	34 CFR 9 Sect. A § 99.3, sect. 8
Directory Information	A specific kind of educational record that would not generally be considered harmful or an invasion of privacy if disclosed. Directory information includes, but is not limited to, the student's name, address, telephone number, email address, photograph, date and place of birth, major, grade level, enrollment status, degrees or honors received, dates of attendance, most recent attendance at other educational institutions, attendance or participation in officially recognized organizations or sports, and weight and height of athletes	A common misnomer is that directory information is not an educational record and that it is therefore not covered under FERPA. Indeed, section § 99.37 of FERPA clearly articulates authority over directory information that simply does not require prior written consent to disclose directory information to any agency or organization.	34 CFR 9 Sect. A § 99.3, sect. 9

(*Continued*)

NEW DIRECTIONS FOR INSTITUTIONAL RESEARCH • DOI: 10.1002/ir

Table 2.1. Continued

Term	Definition	Comments	Statute
Disclosure	Access to or the release, transfer, or other communication of PII contained in educational records by any means, including oral, written, or electronic means, to any party except the party identified as the party that provided or created the record.	To be considered a disclosure, data shared must meet the definitions of PII and educational records. Prior written consent is required for disclosure of educational records and PII.	34 CFR 9 Sect. A § 99.3, Sect. 5

of Agriculture Food and Nutrition Service, state educational authorities, and representatives of state and federal Attorney General offices. Furthermore, a written consent exception is provided to state officials engaged in proceedings in the juvenile justice system and representatives of a Grand Jury executing a subpoena. Specific codes and a number of *Dear Colleague Letters* enumerate the kinds of data and collection procedures such agencies might routinely request or engage in (see U.S. Department of Education, 2016a, 2016b).

Specific external organizations engaged in legitimate operations with an institution enjoy exceptions to FERPA's written consent requirement as well. For example, FERPA affords an exception to "organizations conducting studies for, or on behalf of, educational agencies or institutions for the purpose of developing, validating, or administering predictive tests, administering student aid programs, and improving instruction, if such studies are conducted in such a manner as will not permit the personal identification of students and their parents by persons other than representatives of such organizations and such information will be destroyed when no longer needed for the purpose for which it is conducted" (20 U.S.C. §1232g(b)(1)(F). Accreditation agencies engaged in accreditation processes also enjoy a written consent exception, meaning institutions may share PII with accreditation agencies without prior written consent from students.

Two final written consent exceptions exist that require attention from IR professionals. Considerable debate has ensued about whether or not written consent from a student is needed in order to disclose educational records to eligible students' parents. Confusion has grown as students' college attendance and autonomy patterns have grown increasingly complex. FERPA is clear that "when a student turns 18 years old, or enters a postsecondary institution at any age, the rights under FERPA transfer from the parents to the student" (20 U.S.C. §1232g (4)). Questions arise when high school students are concurrently enrolled in college courses or when students enter college before turning 18 years of age. FERPA is clear that enrollment in a postsecondary institution, in any capacity, triggers FERPA's protections for students' PII (§1232g (5)). Further still, FERPA provides exceptions to the requirement for students' written consent to share educational records with parents when (a) parents claim students as a dependent on their IRS tax claim forms or (b) a student violates a state alcohol or controlled substance law and the disclosure is made while the student is under 21 years of age (§ 99.31(a) 15). Still, many institutions have policies that run counter to this position (Conway, 2016).

Finally, FERPA provides a written consent exception for the disclosure of PII in case of safety and health emergencies. The 2009 amendments were in response to the 2007 Virginia Tech shootings and sought to codify the idea that faculty and staff should work in the health and safety interests of all students if they believe disclosing PII to appropriate institutional officials might avert crises and get students the support or counseling they need. The 2009 amendments made it clear that educators have wider freedom in disclosing student PII without prior written consent if it is reasonable to believe that the student poses a threat to self or others. In assessing the severity of the threat, student information may be disclosed to appropriate school officials, law enforcement agents, and even parents if a *specific* and *articulable* threat has been made by a student. The 2009 amendments also established new definitions of biometric data (such as DNA, retina scans, or fingerprints) as educational records, refined the aforementioned exceptions for disclosure of educational records to institutions to which a student intends to transfer, and reinforced access for parents with students claimed as dependents on the parents' IRS tax claims.

Recent FERPA Developments

Since 2009, political discourses about FERPA have ensued and many clarifications have been issued by the U.S. Department of Education, though no formal congressional revisions have been enacted. For example, in August 2015, May 2016, and August 2016 the Department of Education issued final versions of *Dear Colleague Letters* for school officials of higher education. The August 2015 letter (U.S. Department of Education, 2015) resolved misapplications of FERPA to institutions' medical records for students. In instances wherein institutional health or counseling centers provided medical or psychological services, institutions should follow provisions outlined under HIPAA. The August 2015 *Letter* was a reiteration of joint guidance offered by the U.S. Department of Health and Human Services and the U.S. Department of Education in 2008 that established the longstanding position that, for most institutions of higher education, FERPA will guide most student educational records, including medical records. The August 2016 letter was a final draft of the May 2016 letter aimed at reinforcing FERPA's statutes for sharing students' medical records

New Directions for Institutional Research • DOI: 10.1002/ir

(U.S. Department of Education, 2016b). The August 2016 letter also offered clear language that all IR professionals should heed:

> Most disclosures under FERPA are permissive, rather than mandatory, meaning that institutions choose when to share education records including medical records without consent under the exceptions set forth in 20 U.S.C. §§ 1232g(b)(l)(A)-(I), (K), and (L), (b)(3), (b)(5), (b)(6), (h), and (i). When institutions choose to disclose PII from education records, including medical records, without consent, they should always take care to consider the impact of such sharing, and only should disclose the minimum amount of PII necessary for the intended purpose. (p. 3)

The May 2016 *Letter* (U.S. Department of Education, 2016a) outlined unique challenges and best practices in securing PII for transgender students in light of recent Title IX revisions. In particular, official directory information was scrutinized in light of the unique identity development theoretical stages transgender students undergo. For example, the May 2016 *Dear Colleague Letter* noted that official institutional records and directory information may not align with a student's identity or even name used while in college. Although such directory information can be shared without prior student consent, the *Letter* recognizes that institutions must also afford students an opportunity to amend educational records and request that records not be disclosed.

Penalties under FERPA

Originally, FERPA was enacted to apply only to state institutions of higher education. However, the 1974 amendments expanded FERPA's reach to any institution accepting federal funds under any program. Moreover, the 1994 amendments extended FERPA's provisions to include state education agencies. Conceptualized as such, FERPA is categorized as a Spending Clause statute under the authority of Congress in Art. I, § 8 of the U.S. Constitution to spend funds to provide for the general welfare. As such, funds shall not be made available to any institution unless FERPA's statutory requirements are met.

It is also important to note that FERPA does not create a private cause of action, meaning students seeking redress for a FERPA violation should do so through the U.S. Department of Education's Family Policy Compliance Office, not the judicial system. In *Gonzaga University v. Doe*, the U.S. Supreme Court held that plaintiffs could not sue institutions for damages under 42 U.S.C. §1983 to enforce a FERPA provision since "Section 1983 provides a remedy only for the deprivation of rights, privileges, or immunities secured by the Constitution and laws of the United States" since FERPA is categorized as a Spending Clause measure it would not create a private cause of action under 42 U.S.C. §1983. The U.S. Supreme Court further explained that "FERPA's nondisclosure provisions contain no rights-creating language, they have an aggregate, not individual, focus, and they serve primarily to direct the Secretary of Education's distribution of public funds to educational institutions" (*Gonzaga University v. Doe*, para. 6).

While FERPA does not establish a private cause of action, the Act provides the Secretary of Education with the authority to (a) withhold payments of federal funds under any number of federal programs, (b) issue a complaint or cease and desist order, (c) develop and enforce a compliance agreement with an institution in violation of FERPA, or (d) "take any other action authorized by law with respect to recipient" (20 U.S.C.A. 1234(c) (a)). Still, some courts have tested the theory that the U.S. Department of Education has the right to level suits against institutions to preserve FERPA rights. In *United States v. Miami University*, the Sixth Circuit Court maintained that the Secretary's authority to "take any other action..." "Expressly permits the Secretary to bring suit to enforce the FERPA conditions in lieu of its administrative remedies" *United States v. Miami University* 2002. In the 1996 Miami case, a student newspaper, *The Miami Student*, requested the personally identifiable records from student disciplinary hearings from Miami University, a request the university initially refused. Calling upon the Ohio Public Records Act, *The Miami Student* compelled the university to fulfill the request, though the Miami University Office of General Counsel heavily redacted specific information that made the records personally identifiable. Unsatisfied, *The Miami Student* filed a writ of mandamus request with the Ohio Supreme Court requesting the university submit records with limited redaction of only social security numbers and student names. The Ohio Supreme Court interpreted FERPA broadly, arguing that FERPA did not apply to student disciplinary records because disciplinary records "do not contain educationally related information, such as grades or other academic data, and are unrelated to academic performance, financial aid, or scholastic performance" (*United States v. Miami University* 2002, pp. 958–959), thereby classifying disciplinary records outside of educational records.

Learning of this legal development, *The Chronicle of Higher Education* also filed a request to receive lightly redacted copies of all Miami University student disciplinary records from 1995 and 1996. On July 21, 1997, after receiving *The Chronicle's* request, Miami University notified the Department of Education that it would be unable to comply with FERPA because of the Ohio Supreme Court's ruling and interpretation of disciplinary records as falling outside of educational records. In a response letter dated August 7, 1997, the U.S. Department of Education stated its belief that student disciplinary records are educational records as defined by FERPA. As such, Miami University would be in violation of FERPA if it shared the student disciplinary records. In late 1997, *The Chronicle of Higher Education* also submitted a similar request for lightly redacted student disciplinary records to Ohio State University (OSU), which complied with the request on

NEW DIRECTIONS FOR INSTITUTIONAL RESEARCH • DOI: 10.1002/ir

December 22, 21997. The U.S. Department of Education learned of the disclosure from OSU General Counsel in January 7, 1998, bringing OSU into the legal fray as well. On January 16, 1997, a second, more extensive request from *The Chronicle of Higher Education* was made to OSU, which notified the U.S. Department of Education preemptively of its intent to comply with the request. Consequently, the Department of Education filed a motion for a preliminary injunction on January 23, 1998, with the U.S. District Court for the Southeastern district of Ohio, requesting that all future disclosures of student disciplinary record discontinue. The court found that, indeed, disciplinary records were educational records, contrary to the Ohio Supreme Court's ruling, and that both Miami and OSU had violated FERPA. The Department of Education was justified in leveling any penalty it saw fit.

While the Miami court also held that, "Even in the absence of statutory authority, the United States has the inherent power to sue to enforce conditions imposed on the recipients of federal grants" (*United States v. Miami University*, 2002, p. 808), the Sixth Circuit Court clearly favored a pattern wherein the U.S. Secretary of Education poses the authority to sue institutions of higher learning to enforce FERPA protections. However, the U.S. Supreme Court's determinations in *Gonzaga University v. Doe* revised the jurisprudence on FERPA's authority and clearly articulated an administrative structure for hearing complaints through the Family Policy Compliance Office. It is therefore highly unlikely that plaintiffs will successfully sue institutions in a court of law for FERPA violations although remedies can be sought through administrative structures. To date, no institution of higher learning has been successfully sued in a court of law by individual students for damages to students for a FERPA violation. Moreover, the Family Policy Compliance Office has yet to withhold funds from any institution of higher learning for FERPA violations, primarily because voluntary compliance from the institution is secured prior to legal action or continued violations (Idaho State University, 2016).

Finally, the *Miami* and *Gonzaga* cases spurred a line of cases aimed at clarifying FERPA's parameters. For example, in *Atria v. Vanderbilt University*(2005), which focused primarily on a premed student's claims of negligence in Vanderbilt's finding him guilty of an honor code violation, the Sixth Circuit Court found that FERPA does not support a claim of negligence per se because it does not define a standard of care. Atria alleged that he was harmed by a professor who publicly distributed tests, complete with grades and social security numbers, by making all tests available for pickup by students on a table outside his office. The court found the professor's manner of returning the tests to be unusual at best. Despite chiding the professor for this form of test grade dissemination, the court still upheld his professional capacity to do so, finding that "the harm that Atria suffered does not seem like the sort of harm against which the FERPA seeks to protect" (142 F. App'x 246, 254 (6th Cir. 2005)).

NEW DIRECTIONS FOR INSTITUTIONAL RESEARCH • DOI: 10.1002/ir

Similarly, in *McFadyen v. Duke University* (2011), a North Carolina court found that student plaintiffs may not evoke FERPA to demonstrate sufficient tort claims or enumerate damages. In other words, individual students are not owed a duty of care to prevent the disclosure of confidential data and therefore would not find a fruitful line of redress through negligence claims. Instead, aggrieved students should air their grievances through the established avenue of a formal complaint to the U.S. Department of Education's Family Policy Compliance Office.

Future Developments with FERPA

FERPA has become a framework for addressing a wide range of higher education issues, including sexual assault, transgender students' needs, and campus safety. Thus, FERPA is currently developing in concordance with other statutes such as Title IX of the Education Amendments of 1972, the Violence Against Women Act, or the Cleary Act. The August 2016 *Dear Colleague Letter* (U.S. Department of Education, 2016b) also solidifies the unique interplay between FERPA and HIPAA. One chief difference between HIPAA and FERPA is that HIPAA establishes significant fines ranging from $100 to $50,000 per violation with a maximum penalty of $1.5 million per year for noncompliance with HIPAA. During the 114th Congressional session House Resolution 3157 and Senate Bill 1341, known as the Student Privacy Protection Act, were introduced for consideration. The bill, if passed, would amend FERPA to "prohibit funding of educational agencies or institutions that allow third parties to access student data, unless (a) the institution notifies parents and eligible students of data made available to third party vendors, (b) the institution ensures that data cannot be made personally identifiable, (c) data remain in possession of the institution, and (d) the third party agreed to be liable for FERPA violations" (U.S. Congress, 2016, para. 2). The act also extends to the U.S. Department of Education, in cooperation with the U.S. Department of Justice or the Federal Trade Commission, the authority to levy precisely the same fines noted for noncompliance of HIPAA. The bill came at a time when the U.S. Department of Education, the Obama Administration, and several state agencies faced staunch criticism for security of their student data (Strauss, 2016). The ability to fine institutions for FERPA violations, patterned after HIPAA fines, will further extend the U.S. Department of Education's capacity to enforce FERPA.

IR professionals can also expect considerable discussion on data sharing to continue in light of ongoing access, affordability, and accountability discourses. A recent example of this would include the August 2016 release of *Joint Guidance on Data Matching to Facilitate WIOA Performance Reporting and Evaluation* (U.S. Department of Labor & U.S. Department of Education, 2016). The Workforce Innovation and Opportunity Act was passed in 2014 by Congress to facilitate the training and employment of Americans in high-quality jobs and requires institutions to collect data on wages for alumni.

This presents IR leaders with challenges in accessing confidential data to which they traditionally lack access. Some IR leaders are finding it beneficial to partner with vocational placement assistance agencies or unemployment agencies to track wages of students exiting the college environment and entering the workforce through such vocational placement agencies. These agencies are not considered educational institutions or state education agencies and, as such, are not subject to FERPA. Still, some IR leaders are rightfully hesitant to share educational records with such agencies.

Conclusion

Confidentiality of student data will continue to be a defining issue for IR leaders. FERPA was originally enacted to ensure that "parents and students may properly begin to exercise their rights under the law, and the protections of their privacy may be assured" (Senator Buckley in U.S. Congress, 1975, Rec. 39,863). Through its lengthy history, FERPA has remained the prominent legislative act governing how higher education institutions track students, collect and use data for improvement, and engage in scholarly discourse about learning. IR leaders should look to partner with general counsel and employ a well-informed, balanced approach to preserving student privacy. An understanding of FERPA and institutional rights can lead to a balanced, informed perspective and effective practice.

References

Association for Institutional Research. (2012). *IR professionals' familiarity with FERPA*. Tallahassee, FL: Association for Institutional Research. Retrieved from http://www.airweb.org/eAIR/Surveys/Pages/FERPA.aspx

Atria v. Vanderbilt University, 142 F. App'x 246 (6th Cir. 2005).

Conway, C. A. (2016). Understand how Cleary Act, FERPA, FOIA impact privacy of student records. *Campus Legal Adviser, 16*(6), 6. doi:10.1002/tsr.30190

Electronic Privacy Information Center. (2016). *EPIC student privacy project*. Retrieved from https://epic.org/privacy/student/

Family Educational Rights and Privacy Act, 20 U.S.C. § 1232g (1974).

Gonzaga University v. Doe, 536 U.S. 273, 122 S. Ct. 2268, 153 L. Ed. 2d 309 (2002).

Higher Education Compliance Alliance. (2015, December). *Higher Education Compliance Alliance Matrix*. Retrieved from http://www.higheredcompliance.org/matrix/

Idaho State University. (2016). *General FERPA information*. Retrieved from http://www.isu.edu/registrar/ferpa/

MacDonald, S. J. (2008, April). The Family Educational Rights and Privacy Act: 7 myths and the truth. *The Chronicle of Higher Education, 54*(32), p. A53.

McFadyen v. Duke University, 786 F. Supp. 2d 887 (M.D.N.C. 2011).

Strauss, V. (2015, June 7). Privacy advocates accuse Obama administration of failing to properly protect student data. *The Washington Post*. Retrieved from https://www.washingtonpost.com/news/answer-sheet/wp/2016/06/07/privacy-advocates-accuse-obama-administration-of-failing-to-properly-protect-student-data/?utm_term=.41821d5615d4

U.S. Congress (1975). Statement of Senator Buckley. 121 Cong. Rec. 13,990.

U.S. Congress. (2016, May 14). *S.1341—Student Privacy Protection Act.* Retrieved from https://www.congress.gov/bill/114th-congress/senate-bill/1341

U.S. Department of Education. (2015, August 18). *Dear colleague letter to school officials at institutions of higher education.* Washington, DC: U.S. Department of Education. Retrieved from http://ptac.ed.gov/sites/default/files/DCL%20Final%20Signed-508.pdf

U.S. Department of Education. (2016a, May 13). *Dear colleague letter on transgender students.* Washington, DC: U.S. Department of Education. Retrieved from http://www2. ed.gov/about/offices/list/ocr/letters/colleague-201605-title-ix-transgender.pdf

U.S. Department of Education. (2016b, August 24). *Dear colleague letter to school officials at institutions of higher education.* Washington, DC. Retrieved from http://familypolicy. ed.gov/sites/fpco.ed.gov/files/DCL_Medical%20Records_Final%20Signed_dated_9-2. pdf

U.S. Department of Education. (2017). *FERPA for school officials.* Washington, DC. Retrieved from http://familypolicy.ed.gov/ferpa-school-officials

U.S. Department of Health and Human Services; U.S. Department of Education. (2008, November). Joint guidance on the application of the Family Educational Rights and Privacy Act (FERPA) and the Health Insurance Portability and Accountability Act of 1996 (HIPAA) to student health records. Washington, DC.

U.S. Department of Labor & U.S. Department of Education. (2014). *Joint guidance on data matching to facilitate WOIA performance reporting and evaluating.* Washington, DC: U.S. Department of Labor & U.S. Department of Education. Retrieved from http:// familypolicy.ed.gov/content/joint-guidance-data-matching-facilitate-wioa-performa nce-reporting-and-evaluation

United States v. Miami University, 294 F.3d 797, 808 (6th Cir. 2002).

Matthew Fuller, PhD. Associate Professor, Higher Education Leadership, Sam Houston State University

New Directions for Institutional Research • DOI: 10.1002/ir

3

This chapter outlines the varying threats that IR professionals face when securely storing and managing data, as well as the regulatory structure in place to control data management. Advice is offered on how best to structure and manage student data.

The Legal Implications of Storing Student Data: Preparing for and Responding to Data Breaches

Katie Beaudin, Esq

Institutional research (IR) staff collect vast amounts of data including student demographics and backgrounds, course grades, financial aid, and other personally identifiable information (PII). When vast amounts of data are retained, the amount of risk involved is heightened. Higher education institutions are certainly not immune to these risks. Since 2015, educational institutions have experienced over 30 data breaches that were reported by the Privacy Rights Clearinghouse (Privacy Rights Clearinghouse, 2016). These breaches have occurred as a result of hackers, malware, phishing emails, computer theft, inadvertent release of information, and in some cases, malicious insiders.

Colleges and universities are in the position of collecting, securing, and maintaining data while simultaneously being subject to several specific regulations. Beyond the Family Educational Rights and Privacy Act (FERPA)—and in the case of higher educations with medical or counseling centers, the Health Insurance Portability and Accountability Act, or HIPAA)—each state has its own set of laws relating to data privacy and data retention.[1] In order to be properly prepared for a data breach, institutions must understand what laws they are subject to when it comes to collecting, using, and storing student and faculty data. If a data breach occurs, courts and government agencies will look to data breach preparedness plans and policies as a mitigating factor that lessens the severity of a sentence or penalty levied against an institution. Beyond federal regulations such as FERPA and HIPAA, institutions must understand the intricate differences between each state's data privacy and notification laws. The ability to respond promptly and effectively to a data breach is another mitigating factor. In the unfortunate circumstance that an institution's data are compromised, there

NEW DIRECTIONS FOR INSTITUTIONAL RESEARCH, no. 172 © 2017 Wiley Periodicals, Inc.
Published online in Wiley Online Library (wileyonlinelibrary.com) • DOI: 10.1002/ir.20202

must be an incident response plan in place for notifying individuals and reforming weak systems.

Some institutions may choose to secure and manage data onsite. This requires institutions to determine which employees have access to certain kinds of data. Institutions also must be hyperdiligent about educating employees and ensuring that security systems are up to date. For higher education institutions that work with third party vendors to retain or process data, there is an additional set of considerations. This includes structuring vendor contracts to take into account the possibility of that third party vendor experiencing a data breach. A prudent vendor contract will subject the vendor to the same or even enhanced standard of security that an institution requires of itself. At the end of this chapter, I offer institutions guidance on what laws govern data management and security, and how best to proceed practically and prudently in creating data management plans or contracting outside the institution for data protection and storage.

This chapter begins with a discussion about how data breaches occur. Next, I discuss the laws governing data breach prevention and data breach response plans. Litigation that has resulted from data breaches at higher education institutions is presented. I then address how best to manage data onsite should an institution choose not to contract with a third-party data vendor. In the event that an institution does contract with a third-party vendor, the chapter concludes with recommendations for structuring third-party contracts.

How Data Breaches Occur

Data breaches come in many shapes and sizes, and it is important that higher education leaders understand where their institutions are at risk in order to identify how best to mitigate those risks. The Identity Theft Research Center defines a data breach as "an incident in which an individual name plus a Social Security number, driver's license number, medical record or financial record (credit/debit cards included) is potentially put at risk because of exposure" (Identity Theft Resource Center, 2016, p. 2). Exposure can occur both externally and internally. An example of an external exposure would be a hack or theft of devices that store data. On the other hand, institutions are also susceptible to internal threats such as employees gaining access to data that they are not authorized to access or disgruntled employees using data improperly. Understanding the main kinds of data breaches can help institutions determine best practices and policies for limiting access to data. This section will outline the types of data breaches and the steps institutions can take to limit both the likelihood of a data breach and the potential legal liabilities involved.

Hacking.   Hacking tends to be the most common, and most publicized, form of data breach. Higher education institutions have been no stranger to hacks in recent history. On January 22, 2016, the University of

Virginia experienced a data exposure after unauthorized individuals illegally accessed its human resources system and exposed personally identifiable information for university employees (University of Virginia, 2016). Hackers sent a "phishing" email to employees asking them to provide user names and passwords. A phishing email is an email sent from what appears to be a familiar email address asking for personal information. Oftentimes, phishers will gain access to a supervisor's email address and ask for personal information to be copied to a separate email address.

The first step institutions should take is to have data security policies in place and train employees on the risks of hacking and malware. Because of the increasing prevalence of phishing email attacks, educating employees and students alike is the first line of defense against hacks. If an employee is aware of what a phishing email looks like, then they are less likely to fall victim to a scheme. A phishing email could resemble an external data request, making it difficult for IR staff to distinguish between the two. Encouraging communication between employees and supervisors is an easy way to ensure that phishing scams like that are unsuccessful. Employees should feel comfortable questioning a supervisor's request for more data or increasingly private information, as that is often the main line of attack for phishers.

Physical Theft.   In California, during 2012 and 2013, physical theft and loss of devices accounted for 25% of education industry data breaches (California Department of Justice, 2014, p. 11). In September 2015, a doctor at the LSU Health New Orleans School of Medicine had his laptop stolen, which compromised the personal information of some 5,000 patients. The laptop was taken from the doctor's car while it was parked in front of his home (LSU Health New Orleans, 2015). A laptop computer and media card used by a faculty member at the University of Maine were stolen from a checked bag on an airline flight in early 2015, exposing the personal information of 941 students enrolled in physics courses dating to 1999 (The University of Maine, 2015).

In the event personal information is compromised because of an accident or improperly maintained devices, institutions may face negligence suits from affected individuals. A device that is properly maintained is one that is password protected and has up-to-date virus protection software. Additionally, properly maintained devices should have encrypted files such that an outsider without access to an encryption code would be unable to process that data. Even if IR staff do not store data on personal devices, if they receive emails on those devices, it is possible that physical theft could lead to data theft as well.

As with preventing hacks, preventing physical thefts starts with educating IR staff on best practices for securing devices. This starts easily with ensuring that offices are properly secured at the end of every day, and requiring employees to secure their computers with complicated passwords. That way, in the event that there is a physical theft in an IR office, there is not a major data breach associated with it. Courts and government agencies alike look to the policies and procedures in place for preventing breaches when determining the liability of the institution and whether to assess penalties against that institution.

Vendors.   A recent study found that 63% of data breaches are traceable to a third-party vendor (Trustwave, 2013, p. 3). Several of the larger data breaches that have affected major U.S. corporations have happened at the hands of a vendor. On December 15, 2015, Southern New Hampshire University discovered a breach of student information (Ragan, 2016). The exposed SNHU database contains more than 140,000 records including student names, email addresses, and IDs; as well as other class-related details such as course name, course section, assignment details, and assignment score. The database also contains instructor names and email addresses. The University stated that the breach occurred as a result of a configuration error with one of its vendors. These breaches have significantly affected institutional reputation, resulted in high financial and human resource costs, and have contributed to the Student Privacy Protection Act currently being considered by Congress. If enacted, the Act would make third-party vendors subject to FERPA regulations (U.S. Congress, 2015).

In order to ensure that data is safe with a third-party service, institutions should vet all vendors and make sure the vendor is one that is well known and well regarded. The decision to contract with a vendor should not be a simple one and should involve an extensive auditing process. Once a vendor is chosen, the institution needs to structure the contract to hold the vendor to a security standard that is the same, or greater, than that of the institution. The third section of this chapter will address in more detail the structure of vendor agreements.

Regulation of Higher Education Data

Before determining what practices to have in place to protect and store data, it is important that all members of an institution understand the regulations they are subject to. These regulations shape how we use data, how we draft contracts related to that data, and how we respond in the event of a data breach. FERPA requires written consent from eligible students in order to release personally identifiable information from education records (see Chapter 2 for greater detail).

State Data Privacy Laws.   Beyond the requirements of FERPA, colleges and universities are subject to the data privacy laws that govern the state they are located in. Each state has its own unique data security laws often outlined in administrative, civil or business codes. These laws each have their own requirements as to how to respond to a data breach. Colleges and universities that have a diverse student population with many students from out of state, or out the country, should understand the requirements of the states and countries that the students come from. These institutions should

NEW DIRECTIONS FOR INSTITUTIONAL RESEARCH • DOI: 10.1002/ir

rely on their IR office to provide them with data about the makeup of their student body. The days following a data breach often require the institution to send notice to the affected individuals within a reasonable time. Because each state is different, general counsel should work with IR staff to prepare a data breach response plan based on the state requirements for notification. Following are the requirements under California and New York law. However, it is important to keep in mind that each state's requirements may not align directly with these examples.

California.   The California Civil Code defines personal information as (1) An individual's first name or first initial and last name in combination with any one or more of the following data elements, when either the name or the data elements are not encrypted: (a) Social Security number, (b) driver's license number or California identification card number, (c) account number, credit or debit card number, in combination with any required security code, access code, or password that would permit access to an individual's financial account, (d) medical information, (e) health insurance information, or (e) information or data collected through the use or operation of an automated license plate recognition system, as defined in [California Civil Code] §1798.90.5; and (2) A username or email address, in combination with a password or security question and answer that would permit access to an online account.

Notably, personal information is defined only as information that is not encrypted. Therefore, if an institution encrypts the personal data and the unauthorized access is only of encrypted data, there is no duty to notify. The code specifically requests that "A business shall take all reasonable steps to dispose, or arrange for the disposal, of customer records within its custody or control containing personal information when the records are no longer to be retained by the business by (a) shredding, (b) erasing, or (c) otherwise modifying the personal information in those records to make it unreadable or undecipherable through any means" (California Civil Code, §1798.81). It then goes on to outline its definition of a breach of a security system, which includes the "unauthorized acquisition of computerized data that compromises the security, confidentiality, or integrity of personal information maintained by the person or business" (§1798.82(g)). In the event of a breach, the institution must notify the affected individuals as well as the California Attorney General if the breach affects more than 500 California residents (§1798.82(a, f)). Notice must be given "in the most expedient time possible and without unreasonable delay" (§1798.82(c)). The California statute also allows for a private right of action, so an affected individual could sue the institution following a data breach (§1798.84(b)).

New York.   New York General Business Law draws a distinction between personal and private information. Personal information is "any information concerning a natural person which, because of name, number, personal mark, or other identifier, can be used to identify such natural person" (N.Y. Gen. Bus. Law §899-aa(1)(a)). Private information is defined as

NEW DIRECTIONS FOR INSTITUTIONAL RESEARCH • DOI: 10.1002/ir

"personal information consisting of any information in combination with any one or more of the following data elements, when either the personal information or the data element is not encrypted, or encrypted with an encryption key that has also been acquired: (1) Social Security number, (2) driver's license number or nondriver identification card number, or (3) account number, credit or debit card number, in combination with any required security code, access code, or password that would permit access to an individual's financial account" (§899-aa(1)(b)).

As in California, personal information is defined only as information that is not encrypted. However, New York goes one step further and requires that the unauthorized access also did not acquire the encryption key. That is because if a hacker retrieves encrypted data and the encryption key to unencrypt that data, the encryption is rendered useless. Therefore, if an institution encrypts the personal data, the unauthorized access is only of encrypted data, and the unauthorized accessor does not have access to the encryption key, there is no duty to notify. This highlights the importance of storing encrypted data separately from the encryption key. If a hacker can access both, the encryption serves no purpose. Ensuring that only necessary employees have access to the encryption key is crucial to keeping data secure.

A breach of the security of the system is the "unauthorized acquisition or acquisition without valid authorization of computerized data that compromises the security, confidentiality, or integrity of personal information maintained by a business" (§899-aa (1)(c)). In the event of a breach, the institution must notify the affected individuals as well as the state attorney general, the department of state and the division of state police (§899-aa(2), (8)(a)). Therefore, even if a data breach affects only one student at the institution who resides in New York, the institution is obligated to notify all of the above-listed government agencies. Unlike California, New York does not provide for a private right of action. Affected individuals cannot use the New York state data security regulation to sue the institution.

Private Litigation Resulting From Data Breaches

There have been over 700 data breaches involving educational institutions in the past 9 years, some of which have resulted in class action litigation. Between April 2009 and June 2011, multiple campuses of the University of Hawaii were accused of releasing the private information of 90,000 individuals (University of Hawai'i, 2012). The affected information included names, social security numbers, phone numbers, address, and credit card information. Some of the affected individuals filed a class action complaint against the University (*Gross v. University of Hawai'i et al*, 2010). The University settled the lawsuit and provided the free benefits asked for by the class members. The cost of providing all the benefits was approximately $550,000 plus attorneys' fees and costs (University of Hawai'i, 2012).

In 2013, the Maricopa County Community College District experienced a large-scale data breach involving academic and personal data of 2.4 million current and former students, and employees (Faller, 2013). While the breach occurred in April 2013, students were not notified until November of that year. The compromised information included employee social security numbers, driver's license numbers, bank account information, and student academic information. The Community College District spent $7 million to notify parties and to fund repairs, including the construction of a call center facility. The victims of the breach filed a class action complaint against the Community College District on April 28, 2014 (*Roberts v. Maricopa County Community College District*, 2014). They allege negligence, negligence per se under two Arizona state statutes, breach of fiduciary duty, bailment, breach of the right of privacy, and violation of a federal statute related to the unlawful disclosure of personal information from a motor vehicle record.

In order to prove a claim of negligence, the plaintiff must show the existence of a legal duty to exercise reasonable care; a failure to exercise reasonable care; cause in fact of physical harm by the negligent conduct; physical harm in the form of actual damages; and proximate cause, a showing that the harm is within the scope of liability. In the case of negligence per se, the legal duty is provided by statute. The first negligence per se claim was brought under Arizona Revised Statues, Article 2, §41-4172, which requires the entity to "develop and establish commercially reasonable procedures to ensure that entity identifying information and personal identifying information … is secure and cannot be accessed, viewed or acquired unless authorized by law." The other negligence per se claim was brought under Arizona Revised Statues, Article 2, §44-7501, which establishes "a duty of reasonable care to notify in a timely manner if [personal identifying information] or other sensitive information was potentially exposed to unauthorized access." In December 2015, Maricopa County Community College District's governing board approved a settlement of data breach class-action lawsuits that will offer another year of free credit monitoring to the plaintiffs (Gonzales, 2015).

As is clear from these two examples, many class action suits following data breaches are settled. Therefore, there is little legal analysis provided by the courts on the issue of data breach liability. It is unclear whether courts will in fact hold institutions liable for the loss of personal information because of the tendency to settle such cases prior to resolution. The process of litigating the matter and settling costs institutions a great deal of money. However, mitigating factors such as proper contracts and data policies and procedures reduce these costs.

Storing and Managing Data On-site

Some institutions may decide to process, store, and manage data onsite versus hiring a third-party data vendor to handle data storage and management. The benefits of doing this include increased control over data and the ability to tailor a data plan to the exact needs of the institution. Oftentimes, bringing in a third-party vendor to aid in data storage can lead to increased liability and potentially different philosophies about data protection. If an institution determines that using a vendor is unnecessary, it will need to ensure that proper, effective policies and procedures are in place.

The first step is determining which employees should have access to certain types of data. Not all employees need access to all data types. In fact, keeping data access to a minimum is the best practice for ensuring data is not compromised. Keeping data in silos so that only certain employees have access to varying types of data is a good practice for protecting data. There is a level of trust required between an institution and its employees when it comes to accessing sensitive data. For instance, when an employee is first hired, an institution should not immediately grant them full access to data without understanding whether they are trustworthy. This may mean separating data based on what information is protected by FERPA and what information is simply "directory information." Ensuring that data protection and management are aligned with statutory schemes is the simplest way to ensure that an IR office department does not end up compromising data.

From there, an institution needs to invest in educating employees about the types of data they will have access to and the scope of what they can and cannot do with that data. Institutions could use employee agreements that detail the role the data will play in that individual's employment. This is especially relevant in the case of IR staff who use data for specific purposes. IR offices should work closely with general counsel to structure contracts and understand the broad scope of laws they are subject to. This might include educating employees as to what kinds of data can easily be sent to external parties and which data may fall under a statutory scheme that requires notification or consent in the event of an external data request.

Finally, to the extent that they have them, institutions should also use the resources available on a college or university campus for understanding how best to implement data policies and procedures. An information technology department will be most familiar with the processes employed by the institution as a whole. Additionally, computer science departments keep apprised of the latest trends and threats in the cybersecurity world. Having students and faculty from that department give presentations to an institution's staff on detecting data breaches or weaknesses is an easy way to use on-campus resources. In some cases, institutions may have an ethical hacking club where students experiment with hacking in order to identify weaknesses in computer security. Testing the limits of the institution's security systems will help identify whether data is secure and what next steps an institution should take to ensure that it cannot be compromised.

Trusting Vendors With Sensitive Data

As institutions begin compiling and storing larger volumes of data, it is important that they exercise caution in choosing third-party vendors to aid in institutional practices. This caution starts with properly written agreements. At the very least, contracts with vendors should include provisions governing (1) the definition of personally identifiable information, (2) the level of security required, (3) the procedures in place to detect and prevent a data breach, and (4) a response plan in the event a data breach does occur.

Practical Law Company (2011) provided a great resource for drafting and structuring a data security contract. First, the contract should outline the relevant definitions including authorized employees or persons who will be working with the data. The contract should define personally identifiable information and the type of data being shared. This definition should be broad in scope to cover the various definitions of personal or sensitive information as defined by FERPA, but also as defined by state data privacy regulations. The definition should also take into account potential exceptions to the definition. Even a broad definition may miss certain categories of data, so a prudent contract will contemplate how the parties will act in the case of a new definition that arises in practice. If the data involves information subject to FERPA, the contract should define the specific purposes for which the provider may use the student information. The contract should be clear about the format of the data and how it will be stored. Institutions should know the size, scope, and type of data before drafting the contract to make clear that all aspects of the data are addressed. It should also address ownership of the data and make clear that the data collected belongs to the institution, not the vendor.

Second, the contract should establish the appropriate standard of care for storing and using data (Practical Law Company, 2011). This part should establish exactly what the data are being used for and the regulations that the institution and the vendor are subject to. In the case of student data, it is important that the contract mirrors the language of FERPA. As stated in the earlier section on FERPA, the contract must state the following: (1) the vendor has a legitimate educational interest, (2) the vendor performs an institutional service or function for which the institution would otherwise use employees, (3) the vendor is under the direct control of the institution, and (4) the vendor is subject to the requirements of FERPA [34 C.F.R. 99.33(a)] governing the use and redisclosure of personally identifiable information. The agreement should specify what "direct control" means and how the institution will be overseeing the use of the data.

Third, the contract should establish the security procedures for storing the data. The contract should hold the vendor to the same standard of security that the institution holds itself, if not a higher standard. This will include not only how the data is stored and used, but how long it must be stored and whether the data should be destroyed after a certain amount of time has elapsed. The contract should have a provision that requires the vendor to destroy all data after the contract period is complete so that there is no longer information residing on the provider's system once the contractual work has been completed. It is also important that the agreement include the following provisions: (1) the name and contact information for an employee who is the primary security contact and who is available to the institution at any time to resolve obligations associated with a data breach, (2) the time frame in which the vendor must notify the institution in the event of a data breach, and (3) the information required in a notice to the institution of a data breach (Practical Law Company, 2011).

Fourth, the contract should describe each party's responsibilities in the event of a data breach. This will include notifying individuals whose information has been compromised and notifying the proper federal and state agencies. The contract should also state whether there should be indemnification provisions in which the provider agrees to indemnify the school, particularly relating to a school's or district's potential liabilities resulting from a provider's failure to comply with applicable federal or state laws. Indemnification requires the vendor to compensate the school in case of a failure on behalf of the vendor to secure data. Additionally, the parties should consider whether the institution wants to require the vendor to remedy a violation of statutory requirements and compensate the institution for damages resulting from a breach.

Beyond having strong contractual language in place, it is suggested that institutions do regular reviews of the vendor's security systems. In a March 2016 article entitled *4 Steps to Mitigating Third-Party Vendor Cybersecurity Threats*, Security Magazine said, "It is essential to continuously assess the vendor's security standards and best practices to determine if they meet those of your organization" (Katkar, 2016, para. 11). This includes performing up-to-date patching and vulnerability protection, as well as an auditing or verification program to ensure that the contractual obligations are followed to the letter (Katkar, 2016). Contracts should provide for regular audits to ensure that vendors are keeping up to date with security standards and complying with the contractual requirements agreed to by the parties.

Conclusion

Institutional research professionals should understand how they are susceptible to data breaches before they can take steps to prevent them. IR staff also must understand the federal and state regulations they are subject to so they can put in place proper response plans for responding to data breaches. Most importantly, institutions need to structure vendor contracts to ensure that vendors are properly securing and storing data. Understanding best practices for keeping data will reduce the likelihood of data breaches.

Note

1. This chapter will not address HIPAA, but it is important to note that if your institution has a health or medical center, any collection of that data is subject to HIPAA and the HITECH Act.

References

Arizona Revised Statues, Article 2, §§ 41-4172 and 44-750.

California Civil Code, § 1798.82.

California Department of Justice. (2014). *California data breach report.* Sacramento, CA: Author.

Faller, M. B. (2013, November 27). Maricopa Colleges waited 7 months to notify 2.4 million students of data breach. *The Republic.* Retrieved from http://archive.azcentral.com/community/phoenix/articles/20131127arizona-college-students-data-breach.html

Gonzales, A. (2015, December 8). Maricopa Community Colleges settles data breach class-action lawsuits. *Phoenix Business Journal.* Retrieved from http://www.bizjournals.com/phoenix/blog/business/2015/12/maricopa-community-colleges-settles-data-breach.html

Gross v. University of Hawai'i et al. (2010). D. Haw. Nov. 18, 2010, ECF No. 1.

Identity Theft Resource Center. (2016, Dec. 6). *2016 data breaches report.* San Diego, CA: Identity Theft Resource Center. Retrieved from http://www.idtheftcenter.org/data-breaches.html

Katkar, S. (2016, March 22). 4 steps to mitigating third-party vendor cybersecurity threats. *Security.* Retrieved from http://www.securitymagazine.com/articles/87025-steps-to-mitigating-third-party-vendor-cybersecurity-threats

LSU Health New Orleans. (2015). *Stolen laptop exposes patient information.* New Orleans: LSU Health Sciences Center. Retrieved from https://www.lsuhsc.edu/notice/docs/RothPressReleaseNO.pdf

New York General Business Law, § 899.

Practical Law Company. (2011). *Data security contract clauses for service provider agreements.* New York, NY. Retrieved from http://www.kelleydrye.com/publications/articles/1502/_res/id=Files/index=0/Rosenfeld_Hutnik_Data+Security+Contract+Clauses+for+Service+Provider+Arrangements+(Pro-customer).pdf

Privacy Rights Clearinghouse. (2016, December 9). *Data breaches.* Retrieved from https://www.privacyrights.org/data-breaches

Ragan, S. (2016, January 5). SNHU still investigating database leak exposing over 140,000 records. *CSO Insider.* Retrieved from http://www.csoonline.com/article/3019278/security/snhu-still-investigating-database-leak-exposing-over-140-000-records.html

Roberts v. Maricopa County Community College District, No. CV2014-007411 (Ariz. Super. Ct. Apr. 28, 2014).

The University of Maine. (2015). *UMaine working with information security, law enforcement on theft of computer containing student roster data.* Orono: Author. Retrieved from https://umaine.edu/news/blog/2015/02/18/umaine-working-with-information-security-law-enforcement-on-theft-of-computer-containing-student-roster-data/

Trustwave. (2013). *2013 Global Security Report*. Chicago, IL: Trustwave. Retrieved from https://www.trustwave.com/Resources/Library/Documents/2013-Trustwave-Global-Security-Report/?dl=1

U. S. Congress. (2016, May 14). S.1341—Student Privacy Protection Act. Washington, D.C. Retrieved from https://www.congress.gov/bill/114th-congress/senate-bill/1341

University of Hawai'i. (2012, Feb. 10). *University of Hawai'i Settlement*. Retrieved from http://www.hawaii.edu/settlement/

University of Virginia. (2016, January 22). *Information security*. Retrieved from http://www.virginia.edu/informationsecurity/Jan-22-incident-FAQs

KATIE BEAUDIN, *Esq, Associate Attorney at Stradling, Yocca, Carlson, & Rauth.*

NEW DIRECTIONS FOR INSTITUTIONAL RESEARCH • DOI: 10.1002/ir

4

Institutional research (IR) leaders rely on staff members to accomplish office missions and support institutional decisions. Like any supervisors in higher education, IR leaders must be familiar with a host of employment and intellectual property laws that guide the institution/employee relationship. This chapter offers insights into specific issues IR supervisors and staff members should heed.

A Primer on Employment and Intellectual Property Law: Legal Guidance for Supervisors of Assessment and Institutional Research Staff

William Knight, PhD, Elizabeth Timmerman Lugg, JD, PhD

While IR leaders, particularly new ones, may wish to hunker down and concentrate on their ever-growing project lists, being the leader of an IR office or division means managing and supporting staff members and ensuring that the unit is operating within institutional policy and federal and state law (Knight, 2014). Some scenarios could illustrate how employment and intellectual property laws come into play in IR units.

- An IR staff member with a physical disability informs the Director of IR that she needs Parking Services to establish a parking space for persons with disabilities near the building containing the IR office. Parking Services is not responsive. The staff member informs the Director that this accommodation must be made for her as required by the Americans with Disabilities Act.
- The Director of Assessment informs a graduate assistant in the Office of Assessment that her appointment will not be continued next year due to poor performance. The Office of General Counsel informs the Director of Assessment that he has been charged by the graduate assistant with sex- and race-based discrimination in employment.
- During her performance appraisal, the Assistant Director shares with the Associate Vice President for Institutional Effectiveness that a fellow employee has been creating a hostile work environment due to unwelcome sexual advances.

NEW DIRECTIONS FOR INSTITUTIONAL RESEARCH, no. 172 © 2017 Wiley Periodicals, Inc.
Published online in Wiley Online Library (wileyonlinelibrary.com) • DOI: 10.1002/ir.20203

- The Assistant Vice President for Planning and Analysis is concerned about an ongoing and escalating period of job absences on the part of the IR Analyst. The Analyst has noted unspecified medical issues. After consulting with the Office of Human Resources (HR) and her physician the Analyst applies for and receives up to 12 weeks of leave per year (including unpaid leave) under the Family and Medical Leave Act that cannot result in any adverse employment actions against her.
- After he assumes his new job as Associate Director, a staff member informs the Director of IR and Assessment that he cannot continue permanently with his current H1-B visa and needs the institution to sponsor him for permanent residency.
- The Vice President for Planning, Effectiveness, and Decision Support learns that the Director of Analytics who previously reported to her and has now moved to a new job at another university, has taken a predictive analytic model developed at the Vice President's institution, and is now using it in her new job. The Vice President for Enrollment and Student Success is very upset about this since she feels the use of this tool by other institutions will put your university at a competitive disadvantage and urges your university to sue the former employee for violation of intellectual property law.
- The Associate Vice President for Planning and Assessment is summoned to a meeting with the General Counsel in which he is told that his sharing of surveys and statistical analyses with a group of international visitors to the Office of Institutional Research may have placed the College in violation of export control violations.

These scenarios are not meant to frighten IR leaders, but they are representative of real situations that may arise. IR leader need a working knowledge of employment law, such as §504 of the Rehabilitation Act of 1973, the American with Disabilities Act (ADA), Title VII, and Title IX of the Civil Rights Act of 1964, the Family Medical Leave Act (FMLA), and laws and regulations surrounding H-1B visas/sponsorship for permanent residency. In addition, because IR work includes the creation of reports, databases, and websites, for example, IR leaders need to be familiar with law surrounding intellectual property and export control. This chapter is designed to provide a brief summary of these laws along with some related practical advice for IR leaders.

Employer/Employee Relationships

As supervisors, IR leaders rely on staff and faculty to conduct the important business of IR offices. As such, leadership of IR offices is governed by a number of employment and labor laws. Several of the main federal statutes governing employer/employees relationships are detailed below.

§504 of the Rehabilitation Act of 1973. The first federal law dealing with discrimination against the disabled was §504 of the Rehabilitation Act of 1973, which mandated that any institution receiving federal funds could not exclude any "otherwise qualified individual" solely because of his or her disability from employment. Subpart B of §504 specifically covers employment practices and includes provisions allowing employers to make employment conditional upon the results of a medical examination or the ability to perform necessary functions. Individuals covered by §504 include "any person who (i) has a physical or mental impairment which substantially limits one or more major life activities; (ii) has a record of such an impairment; or (iii) is regarded as having an impairment" (34 C.F.R. §104.3). Individuals meeting one of these criteria are considered "otherwise qualified," and the institution is required to provide reasonable accommodations to allow the individual to participate. Reasonable accommodations may include restructuring the workspace to make it accessible, which might mean rearranging furniture, changing counter heights, or widening doorways, for example. It may also mean changing work schedules or duties to accommodate the disability.

In some instances, because of the type of job or legitimate health risks for coworkers, there are no accommodations that can be made that are reasonable (see *School Board of Nassau County v. Arline*, (1987), or *Chevron U.S.A., Inc. v. Echazabal*, (2002)). For example, if the individual has a communicable disease and there is no assignment where he or she would not come in contact with the public, there may be no possible reasonable accommodation. The employer would then be able to claim an "undue hardship." An "undue hardship" that might throw accommodations out of the "reasonable" range are accommodations that are unduly costly, disruptive, or would fundamentally alter institutional operations (42 U.S.C. §12111(10)). An example might be the inability to install an elevator or lift needed for accessibility in a historically designated building. As such, employers are not required to implement accommodations beyond this reasonableness standard.

The Americans With Disabilities Act (ADA). The Americans with Disabilities Act (ADA) was passed in 1990 and broadened protections for individuals with disabilities previously covered under §504. Just as the Civil Rights Act of 1964 prohibits discrimination on the basis of race, color, religion, sex, or national origin, the ADA prohibits discrimination against individuals because of a disability (U. S. Department of Justice, 2016). Title I of the ADA governs employment while Title III covers places of public accommodation and makes the ADA applicable to any college or university, public or private, that affects commerce and is used by the public. This encompasses all institutions of higher learning.

The ADA covers individuals with a disability, which is defined under the law as a "physical or mental impairment that substantially limits one or more major life activity" of the individual (42 U.S.C. §12111(8)). The U.S. Supreme Court has enumerated the criteria for a substantially limiting physical or mental impairment to include (1) the nature and severity of the impairment, (2) its duration or expected duration, and (3) the actual or expected long-term impact resulting from the impairment (480 U.S. at 288). For example, pregnancy without complications is not considered a "limiting impairment" falling under the ADA because it does not fit the severity or duration criteria. A "major life activity" mirrors those included under §504 of the Rehabilitation Act such as caring for one's self, performing manual tasks, walking, seeing, hearing, speaking, breathing, learning, and working (34 C.F.R. §104.3).

Whether working under §504 or the ADA, before action is required by the institution, there must be actual knowledge of the disability. It is up to the individual claiming the disability to provide appropriate documentation of the disability and its limitation of one or more major life activities. This documentation must be reviewed on a case-by-case basis by authorized institutional officials under institutional policies and procedures that are *neither arbitrary nor capricious*, a legal term meaning a decision is not based on the facts but on the whims of those in power. Once that knowledge is obtained, however, the institution cannot deny a reasonable accommodation or be noncompliant in any other way with the mandates under the law.

Title VII and Title IX of the Civil Rights Act of 1964.   Title VI of the Civil Rights Act of 1964 prohibits discrimination based on race, color, or national origin and allows a federal agency to withhold funding if discrimination is proven. Title VII of the Civil Rights Act of 1964 prohibits discrimination based on race, color, national origin, religion, or sex. The Act was amended in 1970 and again in 1972 to include educational institutions. Title IX of the Civil Rights Act was developed in the 1972 amendments and patterned after Title VI, prohibiting discrimination based on gender in educational programs or activities receiving federal funds.

Title VII is the federal discrimination law most widely used in litigation because of its comprehensiveness and the fact that *disparate impact* rather than *intent* is the standard of proof. Moreover, individual supervisors cannot be held liable under Title VII as institutions are held liable offering greater potential for damages to be paid. Under Title VII, the aggrieved party may bring suit if he or she can show that it was more likely than not that he or she was treated differently than other individuals in his or her place because of his or her race, color, national origin, gender, or religion. This is called presenting a *prima facie case of disparate treatment*. Under disparate impact, the aggrieved person must show that policies that make no mention or reliance on race, color, national origin, gender, or religion, when implemented had a disparate impact on the individuals in one of those protected groups. Furthermore, Title VII allows for a *bona fide occupational qualification* exception. Under this exception, hiring may be based on religion, gender, or national origin if such characteristic is a bona fide qualification of the job (42 U.S.C. §2000e-2(e) (1)).

NEW DIRECTIONS FOR INSTITUTIONAL RESEARCH • DOI: 10.1002/ir

The case of *Lynn v. Regents of the University of California* (1981) established the requirement that any individual claiming discrimination had the burden of proof to make a prima facie case of discrimination in order for his or her lawsuit to proceed. A prima facie case raises an inference of discrimination that then shifts the burden of proof to the employer to show why its actions were not actually a pretext for discriminatory behavior. In cases where disparate treatment is claimed, three elements are needed to establish a prima facie case: (1) that the individual belongs to a protected class, (2) that the individual was qualified for the position, and (3) that despite the individual's qualifications, he or she is rejected.

Title IX of the Civil Rights Act is most often thought of in the context of students; though in 1982, in the case of *North Haven Board of Education v. Bell*, the U.S. Supreme Court held that Title IX does apply to employment discrimination as well. Since the release of the Office of Civil Rights of *Dear Colleague Letters* in 2011 (U.S. Department of Education, 2011), 2015 (U.S. Department of Education, 2015), and 2016 (U.S. Department of Education, 2016), Title IX is now most often connected with sexual assault on campus. In the employment context, both Title VII and Title IX can be utilized as a remedy for sexual harassment, which is seen as a form of gender discrimination.

Under federal guidelines passed by the Equal Employment Opportunity Commission (EEOC) in 1980, sexual harassment encompasses "unwelcomed sexual advances, requests for sexual favors, and other verbal or physical conduct of a sexual nature" (29 FR §1604.11). Sexual harassment can be said to have occurred when (1) submission to such conduct is made either explicitly or implicitly a term or condition of an individual's employment or education, (2) submission to or rejection of such conduct by an individual is used as the basis for academic or employment decisions affecting that individual, or (3) such conduct has the purpose or effect of substantially interfering with an individual's academic or employment performance by creating an intimidating, hostile, or offensive employment or educational environment (29 FR §1604.11).

Types of Sexual Harassment.   There are two types of sexual harassment. The first is known as *quid pro quo,* loosely translated as "this for that." In this type of harassment there needs to be only one action where a person's employment is made contingent upon providing or submitting to sexual activity at the demand of an individual who has an unequal power relationship to the alleged victim. The second type of sexual harassment is a *hostile work* or *educational environment.* To prove hostile environment harassment, a plaintiff must show five elements:

1. The employee or student must belong to a protected class of individuals.
2. The employee or student was subject to unwelcomed sexual harassment.

New Directions for Institutional Research • DOI: 10.1002/ir

3. The harassment must have been based on the individual's gender.
4. The harassment must affect the terms, conditions or privilege of employment or education.
5. The employer/institution knew or should have known of the harassment and failed to take proper remedial action.

The importance of the sexual harassment being unwelcomed by the individual being harassed, even without such harassment having an economic impact on the individual, was emphasized by the U.S. Supreme Court in the case of *Meritor Savings Bank v. Vinson*, 477 U.S. 57, (1986). A plaintiff can establish a violation of Title VII by proving a hostile environment without showing an economic effect or loss of employment. The claim that the sexual relationship was consensual or "voluntary" in the sense that it was not physically forced is not the standard; the standard is whether the sexual advances were "unwelcomed." Sexual harassment situations clearly offer many challenges to IR leaders, and general counsel or HR staff should be consulted prior to and during sexual harassment allegations.

Family Medical Leave Act (FMLA) of 1993. The Family Medical Leave Act (FMLA) was passed in 1993 to provide unpaid leave for individuals facing family or health emergencies and to protect their employment and health insurance coverage. Any public or private employer with 50 or more employees is covered by the law. An eligible employee under the FMLA is anyone who has worked for the employer at least 12 months and has worked at least 1250 hours during the year directly preceding the year in which the leave is taken. Seasonal workers may be covered because the 12-month threshold does not need to be consecutive. Exempted from mandatory coverage are those individuals whose salary falls within the highest 10% (29 C.F.R. §825.103(3)). Under the FMLA an employee may take up to 12 weeks every 12 months for birth or adoption of a child, to provide care for a family member facing a health emergency, a personal health condition, or for an exigency that has arisen out of a family member serving in the armed forces. These weeks are in addition to any medical leave accumulated by the employee through employer benefits programs. When both spouses are employed by the same employer they only get 12 months between them for anything other than personal illness. Upon return, the employee is entitled to the same or equivalent position. (For more thorough discussion, see *Burlington Industries v. Ellerth* (1998) or *Faragher v. City of Boca Raton* (1998)). While the FMLA protects employees from being fired for maternity or health problems, it was also left to the employer's discretion as to whether the leave would be paid or unpaid and whether it would run concurrently or consecutively with the employee's sick leave. Such decisions would be contained in HR policies and employee handbooks.

In addition, an employee must be "otherwise qualified" as defined under the ADA in order to be entitled to benefits under FMLA, which was not the case in *Hatchett v. Philander Smith College* (2001). Hatchett was the business manager for Philander Smith College. While on a business trip Hatchett incurred a head injury that affected her ability to fulfill all of her job duties and the college said that she had to go on full-time, FMLA leave. Hatchett went on leave but continued to work from home on those portions of her job where she was capable. Upon her medical release to return part-time she was told that the business manager position no longer existed and was offered three other part-time positions. She refused all of the positions and the college considered her terminated. She sued alleging violations of the FMLA, the ADA, and Title VII. The appellate court found that since her injury rendered her unable to perform her job duties, she was no longer "otherwise qualified" and therefore not entitled to protection under the ADA. The court also found that under the FMLA, an employee who could not perform the essential functions of her job regardless of whether on a full or reduced schedule, was not entitled to intermittent or reduced schedule leave under the FMLA. Personal or family medical leave can be a complex scenario for IR leaders. Fortunately, HR staff, general counsel, and other leaders can be excellent guides in navigating these challenging situations.

H-1B Visas/Sponsorship for Permanent Residency. IR leaders often supervise staff with international residency statuses. H-1B visas are nonimmigrant visas that allow employers to temporarily employ foreign workers who possess a special knowledge or expertise needed by the employer. Before H-1B visas can be obtained, there must be a bona fide employer-employee relationship and the employer must test the availability of U.S. citizens or permanent residents for the job. The employer-employee relationship is usually determined by whether the employer can hire, fire, supervise, and control the work of the H-1B applicant whereas the availability of U.S. citizens is usually covered via a job interview, though additional examinations of potential applicant pools may be necessary. H-1B visas are capped at 65,000 per year, nationwide. The first 20,000 applications made by individuals with an advanced degree are exempt from this cap, as are any potential employees of higher education institutions. H-1B visas are valid for up to six years, during which time the H-1B visa holder can apply for permanent residency status. Sponsoring an individual for permanent residency requires a substantial commitment of university resources and therefore should only be requested when there is institutional need. Employees on H-1B visas must hold at least a bachelor's degree and related certificates as required. If employment is terminated, an H-1B visa holder must apply for permanent residency if eligible, be hired by another sponsoring employer, or leave the country. H-1B visas and sponsorships may be revoked at an institution's discretion, if funding is not available to support a renewal of the sponsorship, or if a visa holder engages in illegal or criminal activity. IR leaders contemplating sponsoring or revoking an H-1B visa for an employee should engage related staff early in the employment process.

NEW DIRECTIONS FOR INSTITUTIONAL RESEARCH • DOI: 10.1002/ir

Ownership of Property and Work Product

IR leaders face a unique set of policies related to the creation and ownership of the byproducts of IR staff members' work. Though many laws guiding intellectual property have traditionally applied to faculty research, they may also apply to IR staff members' work. Intellectual property and export control laws are reviewed below.

Intellectual Property.   The law covering intellectual property is comprised of four types: (1) trade secrets, (2) patents, (3) copyright, and (4) trademark. All four types of intellectual property are protected by statutory and court decisions. Trade secrets apply to such things as devices, formulas, and manufacturing processes and patterns and are protected by state statutes such as the Uniform Trade Secrets Act. The Patent Act of 1790 is a federal act protecting patents. Literature, computer software, and various artistic endeavors are covered by the federal Copyright Act of 1790. Finally, trademarks are protected under the federal Lanham Act of 1946 (Pub. Law 79–489, 60 Stat. 427) and court decisions dealing with unfair competition. Copyrights and patents are also specifically mentioned and protected under the U.S. Constitution in the Patent and Copyright Clause, Article I, §8.

Under these statutes and regulations the ownership and/or property interest in patents, trademarks, copyrights, and trade secrets are explicitly described. Such is not the same when talking about employee work product, the ownership of which is based on the specific facts of the case and relevant contract law. As a general rule, work done by an employee at the request of an employer in the scope of the employee's work duties belongs to the employer unless the employee is actually an independent contractor. Such work is often referred to as "work for hire" which means that work done is being done by an employee for an employer, not work that the employee has done one his or her own time that the employer now wishes to use. The easiest way to avoid confusion over ownership of work product is to include an "ownership of work product clause" in all employees' contracts. In this manner everyone is on notice that the work being done for the employer belongs to the employer or the employee and avoids time consuming but frivolous litigation later.

An example of a misunderstanding as to who owned work done by a university employee, *Weinstein v. University of Illinois at* Chicago (1986). Weinstein's contention was that as a member of the academic faculty he had a special "scholarly" status that gave him exclusive rights to all his research projects. The university disagreed, stating that his research was a product of his employment and was part of his regular duties at the university. Relying on university policy, the court found that Weinstein's work product fell within the parameters of the policy, which specifically stated that faculty work product, including work that held a copyright, was the property of the university. Weinstein "therefore possesses no ownership interest in the Clerkship program data, analysis or report and no due process rights attach" (*Weinstein*, 866). A key distinction in the Weinstein case is the presence of clauses delineating faculty members' scholarly works as owned by the institution. Absent such clauses, different findings are plausible.

Export Control.   There exists a system of federal agencies within the Departments of State, Commerce, and Treasury regulating the export of controlled items such as software, technology, or services out of the United States. The agencies have developed two types of export control regulations that impact university research and may influence IR practice. The first type of exports are controlled by the International Traffic in Arms Regulations (ITAR), which regulate exports of items intended specifically for military application. As such, these forms of export are generally outside of the scope of IR offices. The second type of export controls—the Export Administration Regulations (EAR)—regulate export of commercial items with possible military applications. This includes such things as computer software, surveys, surveying equipment, and other technology or scientific research that, although not intended for military use, could be appropriated for such. These items are listed on the Commerce Control List Index (Bureau of Industry and Security, 2016) and may require a license from the Commerce Department to be exported

Since the terrorist attacks on 9/11, universities have come under increasing scrutiny to insure compliance with these regulations. It is now mandatory that universities have complete export control policies and procedures in place to avoid running afoul of the law. Exporting encompasses more than just shipping items to another country. It also includes sending facsimiles, uploading or downloading information from the Internet, or transmitting through an email, telephone, or face-to-face conversation. An export can also simply be a research project between a U.S. university and a foreign university or foreign national, even if the foreign national is physically in the United States. As with other legal aspects covered, it is imperative that an IR leaders work closely with institutional colleagues; in this instance, the export control officer.

Implications and Practical Advice for IR Leaders

Effectively managing personnel issues requires a strong degree of emotional intelligence. It is important for IR leaders to keep their emotions in check so as not to further exacerbate a situation and to try to understand the perspective of both the employee(s) that are the focus of the issue as well as others who are involved, such as supervisors, HR staff, and legal staff (Knight, 2014). Equally important is developing a basic understanding of the employment laws summarized here and how they are operationalized at an institution. It is not the IR leader's role to have as much knowledge of laws and policies as HR or legal counsel staff. However, it is the IR leader's responsibility to be aware of what is happening in his or her area, attempt to resolve issues before they rise to the level of policy or legal challenges, and to keep appropriate persons at the institution apprised of the situation.

Campus offices of disability services, HR, and legal counsel are good sources for understanding obligations as an employer under §504 and ADA and for thinking through what reasonable accommodations might be in an IR office's specific situation. Staff members seeking accommodation must make their needs known and the institution must review such requests through its established process. IR leaders must be very careful to hold health information of staff members confidential in such situations. Colleges and universities typically have a designated institutional investigator for Title VII and Title IX charges of unlawful discrimination. It is very important that anyone facing such charges understand campus processes, follow the direction of the investigator, and accurately and fully document all related communications. Again, maintaining very close confidentiality throughout the process of dealing with charges of discrimination is essential.

Dealing effectively with employment issues is challenging in its own way. Documenting interactions with the affected employee(s) and informing them of institutional policy, applicable law, and supervisors' expectations are very important concerning reasonable accommodations and possible charges of discrimination. While FMLA is a welcome protection to the employee, it can be very challenging to the leader who is still responsible for seeing that the unit's work is accomplished. It may also be difficult when other employees view the colleague on FMLA leave as getting special treatment and can challenge the maintenance of cordial relationships within an office. Moreover, procedures for establishing permanent residency for staff members with H-1B visas can be very time consuming for multiple people and very expensive for institutions. The requirement of testing the availability of U.S. citizens or permanent residents for the job of the person seeking an H-1B sponsorship requires substantial effort and can lead to demoralized feelings for all involved. Unfortunately, the work involved in sponsoring IR professionals (who are typically viewed as staff members and therefore face more stringent requirements than do faculty members) and the poor likelihood for success have led many institutions to stop considering employment for persons who have not already established citizenship or permanent residency.

Intellectual property and export control issues are typically not considered within IR until such time as a problem occurs. While IR staff members' work is not usually copyrighted or patented, it would be helpful for everyone if it were made clear at the time IR professionals began or interviewed for their employment that the nature of their work and the products produced represented "work for hire" as discussed above. Work products that are the intellectual property of institutions cannot be shared outside of the institution without permission. While the IR profession encourages sharing ideas (at conferences, in webinars, in publications, etc.), it is important to

NEW DIRECTIONS FOR INSTITUTIONAL RESEARCH • DOI: 10.1002/ir

establish and be clear about under what conditions such sharing is harm-ful to the institution and needs to be prohibited. Similarly, IR has benefited from the sharing of work among colleagues internationally. Many IR lead-ers have been fortunate to be able to host international visitors and even to visit other countries to share their expertise. However, it is important to establish, before visits happen, when such sharing constitutes a violation of export control regulations and how the risk of doing so might be mitigated.

It is important to proactively discuss with staff members who are at-tending conferences, authoring publications, or leaving their positions the general rule that the work done by an employee is the property of the insti-tution and to clarify understanding of what work could be harmful to the campus if shared. Dealing with export control issues is a new area of respon-sibility for many institutions and IR leaders. Ideally colleges and universi-ties have an integrated set of procedures (covering liability, funding, etc.) that come into play when employees travel internationally or international visitors visit campus.

Conclusion

It is interesting to consider that IR leaders may resent spending time deal-ing with legal issues and view this as an administrative burden that takes them away from their "real work" in very much the same way that faculty members may view dealing with IR or assessment. Nevertheless, becom-ing knowledgeable about employment and intellectual property law issues before they are called upon to be involved in their application is an im-portant part of IR supervisors' responsibilities as leaders and managers. IR leaders are urged to think about how they would respond to the scenarios provided at the start of this chapter, to take advantage of training opportu-nities concerning these topics that are provided at their institutions, and to proactively seek out supervisors and institutional HR and legal staff if any of the situations highlighted here could develop. The law and institutional policies are a changing landscape requiring ongoing awareness.

This chapter, other chapters in this volume, and other publications and resources provide IR professionals with both an overview of pertinent legal issues and guidance on helpful campus resources. In addition to the other chapters in this volume, readers are also advised to consult Boon (2012), which provides practical advice concerning compliance with institutional review boards and FERPA, and Luna (2012), which provides additional information about discrimination law as well as a consideration and implications of the fundamental differences between research and the law. Becoming familiar with legal issues is probably not on the list of IR professionals' most enjoyable activities, but the old adage applies: People don't plan to fail, they fail to plan.

References

Americans with Disabilities Act of 1990, (1990), 42 U.S.C. §§ 12101–12231.

Boon, R (2012). Regulated ethics: Institutional research compliance with IRBs and FERPA. In R. D. Howard, G. W. McLaughlin, & W. E. Knight (Eds.), *The handbook of institutional research* (pp. 325–339). San Francisco, CA: Jossey-Bass.

Bureau of Industry and Security. (2016). Export Administration Regulations, Supplement No. 1, Part 774, 2016-11-25. Retrieved from https://www.bis.doc.gov/index.php/regulations/export-administration-regulations-ear

Burlington Industries v. Ellerth, 524 U.S. 742 (1998).

Chevron U.S.A., Inc. v. Echazabal, 536 U.S. 73 (2002).

Civil Rights Act of 1964, Pub. Law 88-352, 78 Stat. 241 (1964).

Faragher v. City of Boca Raton, 524 775 (1998).

Family Medical Leave Act (FMLA), 29 C.F.R. § 2601, (1993).

Hatchett v Philander Smith College, 251 F.3d 670 (2001).

Knight, W.E. (2014). *Leadership and management in institutional research: Enhancing personal and professional effectiveness.* Tallahassee, FL: The Association for Institutional Research.

Lanham Act of 1946. (1946). Pub. Law 79–489, 60 Stat. 427.

Luna, A. (2012). Data, discrimination, and the law. In R. D. Howard, G. W. McLaughlin, & W. E. Knight (Eds.), *The handbook of institutional research* (pp. 340–353). San Francisco, CA: Jossey-Bass.

Lynn v. Regents of the University of California, 656 F.2d 1337 (1981).

Meritor Savings Bank v. Vinson, 477 U.S. 57 (1986).

North Haven Board of Education v. Bell, 456 U.S. 512, (1982).

Rehabilitation Act of 1973, 29 U.S.C. § 794.

School Board of Nassau County v. Arline, 480 U.S. 273 (1987).

U. S. Department of Education. (2011, April 4). *Dear colleague letter.* Retrieved from http://www2.ed.gov/about/offices/list/ocr/letters/colleague-201104.pdf

U. S. Department of Education. (2015, April 24). *Dear colleague letter.* Retrieved from http://www2.ed.gov/about/offices/list/ocr/letters/colleague-201504-title-ix-coordinators.pdf

U. S. Department of Education. (2016, May 13). *Dear colleague letter.* Retrieved from http://www2.ed.gov/about/offices/list/ocr/letters/colleague-201605-title-ix-transgender.pdf

U. S. Department of Justice. (2016). *Information and technical assistance on the Americans with Disabilities Act.* Retrieved from http://www.ada.gov/ada_intro.htm

Weinstein v. University of Illinois at Chicago, 628 F. Supp. 862, (1986).

WILLIAM KNIGHT, PHD, *Assistant Provost for Institutional Effectiveness at Ball State University.*

ELIZABETH TIMMERMAN LUGG, JD, PHD, *Associate Professor of Education Law at Illinois State University.*

NEW DIRECTIONS FOR INSTITUTIONAL RESEARCH • DOI: 10.1002/ir

5

Data continues to grow in both importance and quantity within colleges and universities. IR professionals need to know ways data can create potential legal issues in order to be proactive rather than reactive to these situations.

What Did You Know and When Did You Know It? Data's Potential for Institutional Legal Issues

Timothy D. Letzring, JD, EdD

"What did you know? And when did you know it?" These are common questions used by lawyers and leaders to determine culpability and potential liability in any given situation. This "knowledge" is often wrapped up in data that can create liability for an organization even though no one person actually "knows" the data. Take the McDonald's hot cup of coffee lawsuit as an example. The jury awarded a woman $2,000,000 for injuries to her thighs when she placed the cup of coffee between her legs at the drive-thru window, and the cup broke and burned her. The news of this award became a leading example of what is wrong with the jurisprudence system to the point that *Seinfeld* made an episode poking fun at the concept. But what did the data show?

It turned out that McDonald's was aware of the potential severity of the injury their coffee could cause both to customers and its employees. According to reports on the actual trial, McDonald's had spent over $500,000 to settle prior coffee-burn claims and had not changed its practice of serving coffee at 185 degrees without warning its customers of the danger (Cain, 2007). Expert testimony on burns showed that at 190 degrees it would only take two to three seconds to cause third-degree burns, 12 to 15 seconds at 180 degrees, and 20 seconds at 160 degrees. McDonald's own quality assurance manager admitted that its coffee was not "fit for consumption" when initially served (Greenlee, 1997). In its defense, McDonald's presented evidence suggesting it was simply providing its customers what its marketing studies showed their customers wanted: very hot coffee. McDonald's experts demonstrated that industry standards were similar to theirs when it came to coffee temperature. The defense also pointed to the level of insulation

New Directions for Institutional Research, no. 172 © 2017 Wiley Periodicals, Inc.
Published online in Wiley Online Library (wileyonlinelibrary.com) • DOI: 10.1002/ir.20204

in their cups, along with the special lid to reduce risks of burns (McCann, Haltom, & Bloom, 2001).

So, what did McDonald's know, and when did they know it? The downside of an organization's knowledge culpability is that a single employee's knowledge can be attributed to the organization's knowledge and lead to the culpability. As a result, 700 coffee burns spread out over 10 years and a single employee testifying to the dangers of the coffee was enough "knowledge" for the jury to find McDonald's liable. Similarly, staff across a variety of institutional offices may be aware of information that could contribute to the institution's culpability in a number of legal situations. Therefore, it is necessary to consider what "knowledge" various offices or even an individual at a university possesses that one could attribute to the university if something were to go wrong. Specifically, with the increase in data collection based on accountability and to improve efficiency of student success, this may increase the likelihood an institution had prior knowledge when something goes wrong. This chapter will explore two hypotheticals demonstrating potential liability in two different legal areas using advanced warning systems as the context. The chapter also reviews related court cases to demonstrate additional potential institutional research (IR) related legal issues. Finally, the chapter explores cases and ideas for how institutions can better position themselves against liability.

Academic Advanced Warning Systems

While institutions collect a wide variety of data for many purposes, one of the relatively new areas of increased data collection involves advanced warning systems concerning student academic success. While certainly data leading to potential liability can come from other areas, these warning systems provide some interesting scenarios. These advanced warning systems are designed to detect academic issues early enough to provide support to the students identified, thereby increasing both the students' chances of academic success that would eventually translate into increased institutional retention and graduation rates. These warning systems can focus on narrow or broad traits, identified through research, as predictors of academic failure. An institution may monitor student behavior such as absenteeism, or student characteristics research has identified as predictive of academic failure, such ACT scores.

These programs are becoming important professional development opportunities and products for academic and nonacademic providers. *Academic Impressions* has held several conferences on how to effectively create an advanced alert system to improve student success. Companies have also created software solutions to develop advanced alert systems including add-ons to current learning management systems or stand-alone products like *Starfish Solutions*. The purpose of these advanced warning systems is laudable. Higher education institutions need to respond to the identified needs

New Directions for Institutional Research • DOI: 10.1002/ir

of their students, and take appropriate action to improve measures like retention. However, data can sometimes provide unintended information or knowledge and thus liability. While litigation around IR data is atypical, it is plausible enough that the IR professional should not be surprised, nor find its institution serving as the test case. To illustrate the plausibility, a heuristic example follows with two distinct paths of potential liability.

Academic Advanced Warning Systems: A Heuristic Example

What follows is a fictitious, though realistic, scenario that could occur on any college campus with an academic advanced warning system for its students.

The fall semester has begun and the newly implemented academic advanced warning system is functioning as intended. Most importantly, faculty are actually using it. During the second week of class, the system identifies several students who are placed on the at-risk list. The success coaches trained to respond begin taking action. They contact the students and begin making appointments for academic counseling. During one of the scheduled sessions with the academic success coach, a student mentions feelings of isolation. The student shares that he chose this college because his high school girlfriend had chosen this college, but they broke up just after the semester began. The student is not responding to any of the academic suggestions and also demonstrates mild rage during the session. A follow-up appointment is made between the student and the success coach.

Between the first and second academic success coach session, the student sees his ex-girlfriend with another male student. This does not sit well and the success coach can tell the student is angry and he is not responding to the academic issues they are discussing. Instead, the student wants to talk about his ex-girlfriend and what a traitor she is and that he hopes she is not successful. He even makes a veiled threat by saying, "Maybe I will help her fail – there is nothing for me to live for here."

The knowledge of these events belongs to the institution even though it is isolated to one person. This success coach may not be trained to handle such an issue with a student. This is not suggesting that there is automatic liability if something tragic does happen. The key for the IR professional is to see this all began innocently from the advanced alert system by identifying students as "at risk." IR staff should be aware of the limitations and parameters the aggregating and using of data presents the institution and how negligence claims may arise as a result.

Overview of Negligence

Most legal claims made against institutions that would rely on data like this scenario will fall into some level of negligence. A party that brings a negligence claim against an organization must prove all four of the following elements for a negligence claim: (1) the organization owed the individual some form of duty, (2) the organization breached that duty, (3) the individual was injured, and (4) the breach of duty caused the injury. Each of these is a critical element, since if the plaintiff fails to demonstrate just one element, there is no negligence (Vacca & Bosher, 2003). Moreover, the role of duty is critical in higher education settings today. In this context one must consider when data from an advanced warning system creates a duty to act. In the hypothetical scenario, the institution could be construed as having created a duty to reach out to students identified as at risk by the advanced warning system. The continuation of the scenario creates a potential duty to protect the girlfriend based on the student's statement to the success coach. The extent and limits of this duty and any negligence could be tested in a court of law. Since advanced warning systems are still relatively new, there are no cases directly on point, thus the hypothetical. But there are some tangential cases we can explore that examine the concept of organizational knowledge and the duty that comes with that knowledge of various types. In many respects, the concept of liability around data is not new. Institutions have always had data and, to some extent, exposure to liability from that data. But in the past several years, the amount and detail of that data has grown significantly, as well as the ability of the institution through the efforts of IR professionals to analyze and interpret the data in much more meaningful ways. Data details reveal which students are having difficulty based on an algorithm established in the system. At some institutions only one person may see or understand the data, but, in the eyes of a judge or jury, the institution could still be held responsible.

Without going into too much legal detail, this is the basic concept behind the agency principle. The agent, or in this context the employee, has knowledge, breached a duty the knowledge created, thus leading to a negligence claim. Under the agency principle, employers are generally liable for the actions or inactions of their employees. In the scenario above, the success coach may not be trained to handle such an issue with a student, but a lawyer could argue the knowledge led to a duty to do something, and failure to act is grounds for a negligence claim against the employer.

Related Case Examples

The classic case based on an organizational knowledge scenario is *Tarasoff v. Regents of the University of California* (1976). In *Tarasoff*, a student at the University of California was killed by a patient of a university psychologist. Prior to the murder, the patient had confided to the psychologist his plan to kill the student. While the police were notified and the patient was picked up briefly for questioning, the student was not warned. On appeal, the court ruled that the psychologist's knowledge of this credible threat created a duty to warn the student of the danger. Going back to the first element of negligence, the court found a duty existed because of the special relationship between the patient and the university psychologist. The remaining elements of negligence fell in line.

The duty to warn can arise in many situations beyond a mental patient's confession of a plan to kill someone. Johnstone (2010) points to a legal dilemma a social worker faces concerning a client the social worker knows has a sexually transmitted disease. Which ethical construct does a professional deem primary: confidentiality or duty to warn the clients' partners? Analyzing the line of cases that followed *Tarasoff*, Johnstone focused on *Jaffee v. Redmond* (1996), a U.S. Supreme Court case specifically recognizing that social workers possess a similar testimonial privilege as other mental health professionals. This case meant that, as a general rule, social workers could not be compelled to testify about the confidential communications with their clients at trial. However, the Court made it clear that it could see "situations in which the privilege must give way" (*Jaffee v. Redmond,* at 18). The court used a serious threat of harm to others as its example for overcoming the importance given to confidentiality protection. To assist the social worker in determining when to breach confidentiality, Johnstone developed seven factors to assess the situation:

1. Seriousness of the harm
2. Probability of harm
3. Ability to identify the potential victim
4. Imminence of harm
5. Probability an intervention can mitigate harm
6. Exhausted all other means except breaching confidentiality
7. Is the patient an agent of harm?

Using some of these factors may assist the IR professional in determining in which direction to lean concerning warning an individual or simply telling a supervisor what has transpired. However, these factors, especially the first four, illustrate the wide swath of gray area that exists around these dilemmas of when to break confidentiality.

IR staff generally do not have the level of relationship with individual students or other potential plaintiffs that a social worker or psychiatrist would have. Even in our scenario, the success coach has a level of relationship with the student, but not the level of a professional that would include a confidentiality obligation like a counselor, social worker, or psychiatrist. This relationship level is an important factor for a court or jury in determining the first negligence element of duty. The success coach and IR staff certainly have privacy issues including the Family Educational Rights and

Privacy Act (FERPA), and likely state level regulations as well. However, if case precedent requires a therapist to ignore his/her confidentiality duty in order to warn others of possible injury, then it would stand to reason that those with lower privacy obligations, including IR professionals and a success coach, could face similar requirements.

But there is a potential twist to this initial fact scenario that rests the potential legal issue directly with IR. Instead of a student being listed as at risk, what if the algorithm leaves a student off the list and he or she fails academically? Such a student could argue negligence claiming the university had a system in place to assist students at risk of failing, and the university neglected this student in its process. Some might content this is an expansion on the educational malpractice claim (see Chapter 7). Malpractice is "professional misconduct or unreasonable lack of skill ... with the result of injury, loss or damage to the recipient of those services." (*Black's Law Dictionary*, 1979). As Tokic (2014) recounts in his extensive review of educational malpractice, the courts, thus far, have been unwilling to allow such a claim to move forward. Instead, the courts typically apply the negligence elements to the claim. Because the courts find the duty aspect of the education profession nonuniform, setting the professional duty of an educator, compared to that of a doctor or a lawyer, becomes too difficult and ambiguous. However, if an institution has systematized its processes based on an advanced warning system and it fails to identify a student for the intervention, we now have a more uniform process that better aligns with professional standards. It seems reasonable with the increase in both quality and quantity of data, and the increased consumer nature of higher education, that a court may eventually recognize educational malpractice claims apart from the traditional negligence claim.

A Second Example

Some aspects of an institution's data collecting process could lead to legal issues beyond negligence. What if, after several years of data collecting through the academic advanced warning system, someone demonstrates that a disproportionate number of minority students are being flagged by the system as at risk? For example, if an institution has 18% minority enrollment, but they represent 58% of all students flagged by the advanced warning system for some level of intervention, this could create at the very least a perception of a discriminatory process. When this happens, the algorithm used in the advanced warning system will come under greater scrutiny. Regardless whether a lawsuit is ever filed, the institution would likely face pressure after this information becomes public.

In 2014, the White House issued a white paper on the issue pointing out that the use of big data both had potential for incredible opportunities but also could have detrimental effects on important values of our democracy (Executive Office of the President, 2014). Crawford and Schultz

(2014) examined the potential discriminatory elements big data sets could produce. Their focus was also on the much larger big data models that have proliferated in both private and public sector arenas, and similar to the executive branch white paper, raised concerns around improper uses of the data. Their specific concerns included medical and health privacy implications, Fourth Amendment violations, and due process violations. Barocas and Selbst (2016) carried this idea to the primary constitutional principle around discrimination: disparate impact. Disparate impact emerged from a long line of cases involving Equal Protection claims under the 14th Amendment related to "suspect classifications," which include race, religion, national origin, color, or ethnicity. Discussion of this concept in the higher education format, albeit not brief, are found in the *Gratz v. Bollinger* (2003) and *Grutter v. Bollinger* (2003) cases challenging the use of race in admissions at the University of Michigan undergraduate program and its law school, respectively. In the numerical hypothetical given above, one could argue the advanced warning system is disparately selecting minority students at a rate three times their representation in the general population of students.

Unlike the negligence arena, the U.S. Supreme Court has established a test that assumes a policy or program is discriminatory if it has a disparate impact on one of these suspect classifications. The U.S. Supreme Court created the strict scrutiny test to make it difficult to support policies or procedures that do have a discriminatory effect on these suspect classifications as it applied in *Gratz* and *Grutter*. One primary argument in favor of the advanced warning system is the compelling governmental interest in using the system. In both *Gratz* and *Grutter* the Supreme Court made it clear that creating a diverse student body at the University of Michigan was a *compelling state interest* but that race-based decisions must be narrowly tailored in the institution's decision-making system.

The first hurdle a university must clear for a court to find its discriminatory policy constitutional is the compelling state interest test. The compelling state interest in our scenario is academic success of all students. Yes, the advanced warning system does have a disparate impact on minorities, but the interventions the university provides once a student is identified are designed to assist students to help them succeed academically. Minority students labeled by the advanced warning system as at risk could argue an injury by such a stigma. Students not identified as at risk and not provided the interventions could argue reverse discrimination, the very basis for the claims in *Gratz* and *Grutter.*

The other key concept in testing these discriminatory processes is the phrase "narrowly tailored." The reason *Gratz* and *Grutter* serve this purpose so perfectly is that the Supreme Court found one process unconstitutional, violating the Equal Protection clause, and the other process constitutional. In the *Gratz* case where the University of Michigan's admission process for undergraduates was held unconstitutional, the university's use of race was not narrowly tailored. Briefly, the admission process did not minimize the use of race in its decision-making process. However, the Law School in *Grutter* was using race as one of many factors and utilized a "holistic" approach to its process, meeting the concept of narrowly tailored and therefore constitutional.

Suspect classifications like race receive the highest protection under both the Constitution, and federal legislation has followed including Title VI. But other forms of discrimination could also occur involving gender (Title VII and Title IX), or disability (ADA, Sec 504 of Rehabilitation Act). So any oversampling by the advanced warning system of any protected class of individuals could lead to claims of a discriminatory system that should be monitored and responded to through institutional services

Considerations for IR

When situations arise wherein data could lead to legal issues, there are four key factors one should consider when moving forward with the information. Following Johnstone (2010), the IR professional should first consider the *seriousness of the harm*. Of all the issues, this is key. Of course, the IR professional should also insure the data is accurate, reliable, and valid. As with other areas of jurisprudence, the more serious the potential harm, the more likely a duty to do something exists. Do data clearly single out a group based on race, color, national origin, ethnicity, or some other protected classification covered under discrimination laws (see Chapter 4)? In instances of discrimination, the greater the gap between the percentage of such students in the general population and the percentage of students selected out by the system, the greater the potential for a discrimination claim.

Second, third, and fourth follow Johnstone's recommendation as well. The lower the *probability of harm* and the *imminence of harm*, or the inability to *identify the potential victim*, the reduced duty to act exists. Since IR staff do not maintain confidential relationships precisely as mental health professionals do, Johnstone's first four considerations are the primary ones an IR professional would need to consider. Continuing with our initial success coach example, what would the assessment conclude using those four considerations to the student's statement, "Maybe I will help her fail – there is nothing for me to live for here." The comment by the student was fairly vague, so we are not sure about the seriousness of the potential harm. But we can identify the potential victims. We have a threat to the former girlfriend ("help her fail.") and potential self-harm ("nothing for me to live for here."). Probability of harm would be based on additional context that is too difficult to put in a hypothetical; specific mannerisms or body language, for example. The success coach likely has some duty to help this student, while there may not be a legal duty to warn. In this situation, unlike the psychiatrist in *Tarasoff*, there is no breach of confidentiality if the girlfriend is warned that her ex is angry.

NEW DIRECTIONS FOR INSTITUTIONAL RESEARCH • DOI: 10.1002/ir

What if the data show a high seriousness, probability, and imminence of harm to an individual that is identifiable? What action should IR staff take? To whom does one reveal this information? While this may depend on one's level of authority and role within the institutional structure, the primary course of action is to inform the immediate supervisor. Unless your supervisor is somehow implicated in the issue, in most cases simply reporting the information to a superior would suffice in meeting the initial obligation of the employee, but the institution could still be held liable. This action by the IR professional also increases the level of knowledge of the institution, but it also gets the information to someone who can act directly on the situation, inform their counterpart in the appropriate area, and/or inform their supervisor or legal counsel.

One caveat involves reporting information to legal counsel. Every employee of a college or university should understand that legal counsel primarily works for the university, not its employees. Bringing the issue directly to legal counsel may not always be in the employee's best interest as employees are not legal counsel's primary client. In fact, depending on what is revealed, legal counsel could perceive the employee as a future plaintiff against the institution. This is not to say that speaking with institution legal counsel is always a bad idea, but knowing their main role is key.

For the second scenario, discrimination, as evidenced by the "disparate impact" of the advanced warning system, is considered harmful by its nature. That is why the courts tend to assume a governmental organization has violated the Equal Protection Clause when it has discriminated based on one or more of the protected classifications (see Chapter 4). While a true Equal Protection clause claim only applies to governmental entities, most private institutions will fall under some level of discrimination protection that applies to all institutions accepting federal financial aid or other federal dollars. As discussed above, defending the process will require demonstrating that the positive aspects outweigh any potential negatives. Just as the University of Michigan Law School (*Grutter*, 2003) successfully argued that using race as one of many factors in its admission process helped provide a diverse student body, an institution could make similar compelling reasons for the way the advanced warning system is operating. But if data shows a clear oversampling of a particular class of student, it would behoove the IR professionals to at least examine the algorithm used to make this selection and ensure that recommendations for the improvement of programs are formulated and enacted. Courts would want to see the application and refinement of the advanced warning system to be as narrow as possible in discriminating against students of particular ethnic backgrounds or genders. Thus, making sure the warning system's algorithm does not have a code or classification unnecessarily causing oversampling is key.

Admittedly, IR professionals rarely find themselves in the position of defending an institution's decision. That is not the primary duty of IR staff. Even more rare is the IR professional being the employee who is the basis for the institution facing liability. But as institutions collect more and more data in response to the many accountability measures, institutional researchers need to understand the same data they know can be attributed to the institution's knowledge. If knowledge is the key concept, then communication is second: having a clear process of communicating information to supervisors first, and then to other leaders so they are appropriately aware of data. The main issue in these cases is when a leader is surprised by what data show. Institutional leaders may never have actually known, but data were present and lawyers for plaintiffs will always argue institutional leaders should have known. Therefore, IR staff should work to ensure that they have the necessary relationships and processes in place to communicate with a broad range of institutional leaders to communicate concerns noticed in data. Such crossorganizational communication patterns are not just legally sound practices but also good practice in IR.

Conclusion

Without question, IR staff and data they provide are critical to many areas of an institution's success. From accreditation efforts to student success tracking, these data sets provide a myriad of opportunities for an institution to improve its processes. But there is always a potential for legal issues when dealing with institutions, and data are no different. While the examples provided do not fit the traditional patterns for lawsuits, our society's increasing dependence on data combined with a growing concern over privacy issues creates a potential framework for litigation. It is better to be prepared than to be surprised; everyone hates a surprise lawsuit.

References

Barocas, S., & Selbst, A.D. (2016). Big data's disparate impact. 104 Calif. L. Rev., 671.

Black's Law Dictionary, 5th ed. (1979). St. Paul, MN: West Law.

Cain, (2007). And now the rest of the story ... about the McDonald's coffee lawsuit. Houston Lawyer, 45, 24–30.

Crawford, K., & Schultz, J. (2014). Big data and due process: Toward a framework to redress predictive privacy harms. 55 B.C. L. Rev., 93.

Executive Office of the President. (2014). Big data: Seizing opportunities, preserving values. http://www.whitehouse.gov/sites/default/files/docs/big_data_privacy_report_5.1.14_final_print.pdf

Gratz v. Bollinger (539 U.S. 244, 2003).

Greenlee, M. B. (1997). Images, issues, and idols in the debate over tort reform. Capital University Law Review, 26, 701–738.

Grutter v. Bollinger (539 U.S. 306, 2003).

Jaffee v. Redmond (518 U.S. 1; 116 S. Ct. 1923; 135 L. Ed. 2d 337, 1996).

Johnstone, G. L. (2010). A social worker's dilemma when a client has a sexually transmitted disease: The conflict between the duty of confidentiality and the duty to warn sexual partners. University of Louisville Law Review, 49, 111.

McCann, M., Haltom, W., & Bloom, A. (2001). Java jive: Genealogy of a juridical icon. University of Miami Law Review, 56, 113–178.

Tarasoff v. Regents of the University of California (551 P.2d 334 Cal., 1976).

Tokic, S. (2014). Rethinking educational malpractice: Are educators rock stars? *BYU Educ. & L.J. 2014*, 105–133.

Vacca, R.S., & Bosher, W.C. (2003). *Law and education: Contemporary issues and court decisions*. Newark, NJ: Matthew Bender.

TIMOTHY D. LETZRING, Dean, College of Education and Human Services, Texas A&M University–Commerce.

6

This chapter provides an overview of the purpose, history, and process of accreditation and a context for understanding the legal considerations of accreditation.

The Evolving Nature of Higher Education Accreditation: Legal Considerations for Institutional Research Leaders

Julee T. Flood, JD, PhD, Jeff Roberts, MA

Accreditation represents an expensive process in terms of time, resources, and money (Alstete, 2007; Vanderbilt, 2015a, 2015b). Some have argued that accreditation also impacts institutional freedom, as colleges and universities must respond to shifting requirements and standards of their accrediting bodies (Cohen & Kisker, 2010). Opinions vary, however, with others advocating for accreditation's value (Wheelan & Elgart, 2015). Although public protection functions have been imposed on accreditation agencies in the latter half of the 20th century, accreditation's historical purposes to protect students and to promote institutional quality generally remain. Accreditation serves as a tool for promoting institutional improvement and excellence (Bloand, 2001; Lubinescu, Ratcliff, & Gaffney, 2001; Wheelan & Elgart, 2015). It is viewed as a mark of quality for an institution, degree, or credential (Cohen & Kisker, 2010). Finally, it also helps facilitate student transfer between institutions (Alstete, 2007).

Institutional stakes are high when it comes to accreditation. Historically, the relationship between accreditors and institutions has been viewed as voluntary (Alstete, 2007; Bloand, 2001; Cohen & Kisker, 2010; Lubinescu et al., 2001) with institutions participating in the process to gain an agency's stamp of approval. Unaccredited institutions are often viewed by the general public as being of lower quality than accredited peers (Alstete, 2007). Additionally, as accreditation has become key to accessing federal funds, lack of accreditation can have a negative financial impact on an institution (Alstete, 2007; Cohen & Kisker, 2010).

In circuitous fashion, an accrediting agency seeks recognition by the government; the recognized agency accredits an institution; and the government then relies on the accreditor's approval of the institution in order for federal student loan funds to be granted to, or expended at, the

NEW DIRECTIONS FOR INSTITUTIONAL RESEARCH, no. 172 © 2017 Wiley Periodicals, Inc.
Published online in Wiley Online Library (wileyonlinelibrary.com) • DOI: 10.1002/ir.20205

institution (Molinero, 2013). As protectors of public dollars, accrediting agencies have thus become connected to the federal government. The ever-increasing entwinement between these so-called private agencies and the federal government suggests that the voluntary nature of accreditation is waning (Alstete, 2007; Cohen & Kisker, 2010). The loss of accreditation may, in fact, prove fatal to an institution (Gaston, 2014).

Institutions contesting adverse accrediting decisions have created a rich body of case law grounded in contractual, antitrust, constitutional, and other legal claims (e.g., Capone, 2009; Fuller & Lugg, 2012). Courts have largely declined certain claims, particularly those with constitutional underpinnings, explaining that such claims are inappropriate against private actors (e.g., *Parsons College v. NCACSS*, 1967). However, institutions' near-universal reliance on federal funding calls the private nature of accrediting agencies into question (Alstete, 2007; Cohen & Kisker, 2010; Flood & Dewhirst, 2014). This emerging concept of accreditors as governmental actors raises constitutional considerations.

This chapter initially reviews the formative history of regional accreditation to demonstrate how the once-voluntary system has become a near-mandatory system of recognition and regulation. Although the earliest origins of American accreditation can be traced to the late 18th century (Gaston, 2014), the focus will be on key 20th-century moments influencing regional accreditation's development. This will show how the role of accreditation has evolved from being a mark of institutional quality to being what has been described as a "powerful shadow government" (Cohen & Kisker, 2010, p. 521). The historical context undergirds the discussion of case law and its development. A better grasp of legal considerations will benefit institutional research (IR) practitioners, whether they are contesting an adverse accreditation decision, defending disputes, or just developing an understanding of accreditation's role and future.

Historical Origins and Public Purpose of Accreditation

The origins of higher education accreditation in the United States trace back to 1784 when the Regents of the University of the State of New York was established as a governing board for what was then King's College, now Columbia, and for other institutions in New York (Alstete, 2007; Gaston, 2014). Although the standards and methods for review were not defined, this set the precedent for oversight of higher education (Gaston, 2014). The expansion of higher education oversight would be limited, however, for the next 70 years. Eventually, other states moved to provide governance (i.e., Iowa, 1846; Utah, 1896; Washington, 1909; Virginia, 1912; Maryland, 1914) (Gaston, 2014). In 1847, the first specialized accreditation system, The American Medical Association, was founded (Alstete, 2007; Cohen & Kisker, 2010); although, that organization would not exert any real influence upon the discipline until the early 20th century (Alstete, 2007).

NEW DIRECTIONS FOR INSTITUTIONAL RESEARCH • DOI: 10.1002/ir

Since the mid-20th century, accreditation has also served as a gate-keeper for institutional access to federal aid dollars (Bloand, 2001; Gaston, 2014; Thelin, 2011), a role that Gaston (2014) said "some find ... inappropriate for non-government higher education accreditation" (p. 38). However, Gaston (2014) noted that accreditation agencies complete "this unasked-for mission effectively and that its assignment to some untried or already overburdened agency would be fraught with risk" (p. 38). This role marked a fundamental change to the nature of accreditation, forever blurring the lines between private accreditation agencies and the federal government (Cohen & Kisker, 2010). As Bloand (2001) noted, "the federal government has had a tendency to over-regulate and to awkwardly try to use accrediting agencies as enforcers of federal law" (p. 23). The potential effect of these changes will be explored later in this chapter.

From 1944 to 1965, four key legislative acts impacted the relationship between accreditation and the federal government:

1. Servicemen's Readjustment Act of 1944, better known as the G.I. Bill (Cohen & Kisker, 2010; Flood & Dewhirst, 2014; Fuller, 2014; Gaston, 2014; Thelin, 2011)
2. Veterans' Readjustment Act of 1952 (Bloand, 2001; Cohen & Kisker, 2010; Fuller, 2014)
3. National Defense Education Act (NDEA) of 1958 (Fuller, 2014)
4. Higher Education Act (HEA) of 1965 (Bloand, 2001; Fuller, 2014; Gaston, 2014)

The effect of these acts has been to link accreditation and the federal government through the mechanism of federal financial aid.

The G.I. Bill was instrumental in expanding access to higher education for millions of returning American soldiers by providing federal aid for education and training. Between 1944 and 1954, student enrollment in higher education doubled (Fuller, 2014; Synder, 1993). At the peak of the original G.I. Bill in 1947, 49% of college attendees were veterans (U.S. Department of Veterans Affairs, 2016). Existing colleges and universities saw surges in enrollment, and new institutions—many of dubious quality—formed to take advantage of this windfall in federal dollars (Fuller, 2014).

The U.S. government attempted to correct some of these issues with the passage of the Veterans' Readjustment Act of 1952, seeking to give funds only to institutions of acceptable quality. Rather than creating a government-run system for evaluating institutional quality, Congress relied upon the existing accreditation system (Bloand, 2001; Cohen & Kisker, 2010; Fuller, 2014). The U.S. Commissioner for Education was charged with creating a list of approved accreditation agencies, and only institutions accredited by one of these recognized agencies could then receive federal funds (Cohen & Kisker, 2010). Bloand (2001) noted, "With the 1952 act, the federal government began a pattern of reliance on nongovernmental accreditation that was repeated in all the subsequent aid-to-education acts" (p. 24).

This pattern was repeated with the NDEA as that Act expanded both college access (Fuller, 2014) and the connection between federal aid dollars and accreditation. The NDEA also included provisions ensuring federal money went to quality institutions. To be eligible to receive funds, institutions had to either be

> accredited by a nationally recognized accrediting agency or association or, if not so accredited, [be] an institution whose credits are accepted, on transfer, by not less than three institutions which are so accredited, for credit on the same basis as if transferred from an institution so accredited. (NDEA, 1958, p. 1582)

Although accreditation was not an absolute requirement for institutions to receive NDEA funds, the Act further strengthened the relationship between accreditation and the federal government through federal aid.

The linking was fully accomplished through the HEA, which expanded federal financial aid to eligible students. As with the Veterans' Readjustment Act of 1952 and the NDEA, the HEA used the existing accreditation system to ensure institutional quality by making accreditation a requirement for receiving any Title IV funds (HEA, 1965). These connections have only strengthened with each reauthorization of the HEA (Gaston, 2014).

The Legal Foundations of Accreditation

Obtaining and keeping accreditation can be difficult. When faced with an adverse accrediting action, institutional leaders may choose to dedicate resources to regaining accreditation or to contesting the adverse action. Agency rules drive the process for contesting an adverse accrediting action, and the likelihood of institutional success is greatest against an accreditor that has clearly violated its own policies and procedures. Institutional representatives should look to an agency's by-laws and any agreements between the agency and the institution to determine the process of appeal. If an institution cannot obtain relief through the accreditor's processes, the court system is the next step in contesting an adverse decision. Courts will first determine whether an institution has "exhausted" agency-provided remedies (e.g., *Sojourner-Douglass College v. MSACS*, 2015).

Courts have acknowledged that losing accreditation can be devastating, stating in one case that "the loss of accreditation would work substantial and irreparable harm to the College" (*Parsons College*, 1967, p. 69), and in another, that it would likely cause the institution to "promptly [go] out of business" (*Chicago School of Automatic Transmissions v. AACSC*, 1994, p. 448). Yet, lawsuits against accreditors are rarely successful for higher education institutions. First, the formative history of the accreditation system

NEW DIRECTIONS FOR INSTITUTIONAL RESEARCH • DOI: 10.1002/ir

has allowed accreditors to develop extensive processes using peer evaluators with educational expertise (Lubinescu et al., 2001). Second, deference is afforded to accreditors because courts (1) respect the autonomy of higher education and are not well suited to intervene in the complexities of academic decision-making (Leas, 1991) and (2) tend to defer to administrative interpretations of law (Scalia, 1989).

Likewise, courts have deemed the actions of private associations not well suited to judicially announced principles or to statutes (e.g., *Marjorie Webster Junior College v. MSACSS*, 1969; *Parsons College*, 1967). Instead, courts have typically limited their inquiries to whether the rules of the association were followed. The *Parsons College* (1967) court hesitated to intervene in the accreditation process, valued peer review for setting high standards, and noted that "judicial intrusion" would not enhance the "public benefits" (p. 74).

Although noninterference in private, voluntary associations has been the courts' general perspective, it is not an absolute. The *Marjorie Webster* (1969) court noted an exception would exist "when the association enjoys monopoly power in an area of vital public concern," and explained that "[i]f the power, because of public reliance upon it, is great enough to make membership a necessity for successful operation, judicial intervention may be justified" (*Marjorie Webster*, 1969, p. 469). Other courts have indicated a willingness to evaluate accreditors' decisions (e.g., *Parsons College*, 1967; Kaplin, 1969).

Applicable Law

Determining which law applies to contesting accrediting agencies' decisions has proved challenging for courts. In *Parsons College* (1967), the college sued its accreditor to prevent a withdrawal of accreditation. The court expressed that "[t]he controversy presents novel and far-reaching questions concerning the law governing accreditation and the role of the courts in that evaluative process" (*Parsons College*, 1967, p. 65). After acknowledging the harm a loss of accreditation would bring, the court explained "[t]he governing law lies outside the Constitution" (*Parsons College*, 1967, p. 70). Neither was Illinois law governing such actions "wholly free from uncertainty," where the courts had left members to "arrange their affairs as they choose" and bound by the rules of the association (*Parsons College*, 1967, p. 70).

Contract Law.   Institutional leaders typically sign a plethora of agreements with an accreditor when beginning the accreditation process. Despite commercial-like procedures involved, such as paying membership dues and attending business meetings, courts have not generally deemed these seemingly contractual relationships to be contractual. Whereas contract formation requires a bargained-for exchange, the accreditation system is based in a set of rules and regulations. The court in *Professional Massage Training*

New Directions for Institutional Research • DOI: 10.1002/ir

Center v. AACSC (2015) opined that applying for accreditation and using accreditation standards do not create a binding contract since "the [accreditor] can alter the alleged 'contract' at will" and is "thus ... not bound by its terms" (p. 181). Contract principles have also been deemed not to apply because accrediting agencies "are not engaged in commercial transactions for which state-law contract principles are natural matches" (*Chicago School*, 1994, p. 449).

Antitrust Law. Accreditation disputes are not well matched to antitrust suits largely because of questions regarding whether institutions engage in trade, whether students are consumers, whether accreditors restrict trade, and whether there is noncompetitive intent in accreditors' requisites. In *Marjorie Webster* (1969), the junior college's request for regional accreditation was denied based on the institution's for-profit status. The college brought the action, in part, under the provision of § 3 of the Sherman Antitrust Act of 1890 (2012), arguing that the accreditor "acquired monopoly power over regional accreditation" and "unreasonably exercise[d] this power in such a manner as to prevent or inhibit competition from proprietary institutions" (*Marjorie Webster*, 1969, p. 462). Finding the question of antitrust violation "new and pivotal" (*Marjorie Webster*, 1969, p. 465), the court concluded the institution's trade had been "unreasonably restrained" (p. 471). Commonly, though, antitrust violations are not found in accrediting suits (e.g., *Massachusetts School of Law at Andover v. ABA*, 1998).

Constitutional Law and State Actors. Generally, a state actor is someone who acts on behalf of a governmental entity. When doing so, the actor is subject to regulation under the United States Constitution, in particular the First, Fifth, and Fourteenth Amendments. These amendments serve to protect people from governmental violations of certain rights and freedoms. Any party that seeks to claim constitutional violations of this type must explain how a government actor infringed upon their rights.

State actors are subject to constitutional due process standards. "[I]t is well settled that the fourteenth amendment proscription against deprivations of property without due process of law reaches only government action and does not inhibit the conduct of purely private persons in their ordinary activities" (*Jeffries v. GRFA*, 1982, p. 922). Plainly, "[d]ue process does not exist between private actors" (*Auburn University v. SACS*, 2002, p. 1370). Perplexing, then, is courts' application of due process requisites—a standard usually reserved for governmental actors—to ostensibly "private" and "voluntary" accrediting agencies.

Due Process. Due process is an area where institutions may successfully challenge adverse accrediting actions (e.g., *Auburn University*, 2002). In disputes between institutions and their accreditors, courts have consistently held that an accreditor's actions must conform to "fundamental principles of fairness" (e.g., *Medical Institute of Minnesota v. NATTS*, 1987, p. 1314; *Thomas M. Cooley Law School v. ABA*, 2006, p. 713). The presumption that due process standards apply to accreditors has historical roots. The Seventh Circuit explained in 1938 that accreditation decisions would not be upheld if "arrived at arbitrarily and without sufficient evidence" (*North Dakota v. NCACSS*, 1938, p. 700). In *Parsons College* (1967), though the court denied the applicability of constitutional due process and was somewhat dismissive of the college's claim that "rudimentary due process" applied, it nonetheless examined whether the college had received a hearing and was put on notice of its claims (p. 72).

Due process is a "flexible concept" varying with facts presented by a particular case (*Auburn University*, 2002, p. 1374). Lacking clear parameters of fairness, a reviewing court will balance the seriousness of the action against the provided procedural safeguards (*Edward Waters College v. SACS*, 2005). Using accreditation procedures as guides for assessing unique circumstances presented by institutions, courts have deemed "fair" to mean similar, not identical, treatment by similarly situated schools (Capone, 2009; *Medical Institute*, 1987).

Although complex, due process does have distillable components (Capone, 2009). The standard requires that an accrediting agency's decision must not be arbitrary and capricious, and that a plaintiff must receive adequate notice and opportunity to be heard (*Rockland Institute v. AICS*, 1976). The arbitrary and capricious standard is rarely used as the basis for a court's decision against an accreditor because review requires examining substantive professional decisions. Conversely, the process-based nature of the "notice and opportunity to be heard" component requires no subject area expertise; thus, courts are more willing to evaluate the adequacy of an accreditor's process (Capone, 2009). Accrediting agencies do have discretion, but when faced with an adverse accrediting action, institutional leaders should determine whether an accreditor followed legal principles and their own policies and procedures.

Public/Private Dichotomy and Government Entwinement.   Incongruent labels and complex judicial reasoning underscore uncertainties about accreditors' public/private status. The *Chicago School* (1994) court explained the accreditor served a public function, the institution "wanted a key that would unlock the federal Treasury," and an "accrediting agency is a proxy for the federal department whose spigot it opens and closes" (p. 449). Belying the "proxy" label it imposed, the court footnoted that it sought *not* "to imply that an accrediting agency is a 'state actor' or a 'federal actor' with special constitutional obligations in addition to those created by statutes and common law" (*Chicago School*, 1994, p. 449). After confusingly connecting and then disconnecting the agency and the government, the court nonetheless applied federal administrative law to review the institution's claims.

The *Professional Massage* (2015) Court said accreditors have a "quasi-public nature" and serve a "quasi-public role," yet deemed them "private entities" (p. 171). But whether accrediting agencies have been labeled

NEW DIRECTIONS FOR INSTITUTIONAL RESEARCH • DOI: 10.1002/ir

"private" (*Professional Massage*, 2015, p. 169), "quasi-governmental" (*Marjorie Webster*, 1969, p. 462), "quasi-public" (*Auburn University*, 2002, p. 1373; *Cooley*, 2006, p. 711), or public bodies subject to state action analysis (*Brentwood Academy v. TSSAA*, 2001, p. 933; *St. Agnes Hospital of the City of Baltimore v. Riddick*, 1987, p. 481), courts have imposed a common law duty upon accreditors to employ due process procedures when making decisions affecting their members.

The *Auburn University* (2002) court noted the increased involvement of the federal government with the passage of the HEA of 1965, and recounted testimony from an executive director of accrediting agencies who stated that "accrediting organizations have been enticed to become reluctant extensions of the U.S. Office of Education in order that the accredited schools, programs, and colleges might share in the largesse writ large" (p. 1368). Noted the court, with "membership in private associations a 'virtual prerequisite' to the practice of a given profession," increased government involvement in accreditation aligned with courts developing a theory of "common law due process" to which higher education institutions are "entitled" (*Auburn University*, 2002, p. 1369). Calling common law due process a "peculiar body of law," since "[d]ue process does not exist between private parties," the court confronted the public/private tension:

> Although courts consistently stress that accrediting agencies are 'private' actors ... they have felt compelled to apportion some kind of public attribute to these agencies presumably because the agencies have become the gatekeeper to federal financial aid funds without which schools would be unable to function ... Yet courts seem equally compelled to deny that accrediting agencies are state actors. (*Auburn University*, 2002, pp. 1370–1371)

Even prior to the full enmeshing of accreditation and federal dollars, courts assessed whether the government/accreditor relationship rose to the level of the accreditor being considered a state actor (e.g., *Marjorie Webster*, 1969). Three Supreme Court cases unrelated to accreditation have informed subsequent state action decisions. In one, the Court explained that acts of private companies do not become acts of the government because of their significant or even total engagement in performing public contracts, but rather the public function exception considers whether such actions are "traditionally the *exclusive* prerogative of the State" (*Rendell-Baker v. Kohn*, 1982, p. 842). In another, the Court explained that "a State normally can be held responsible for a private decision only when it has exercised coercive power or has provided such significant encouragement, either overt or covert, that the choice must in law be deemed to be that of the State" (*Blum v. Yaretsky*, 1982, p. 1005). The Court explained in a third case that state action is present if the action of a private entity is "fairly attributable" to the State or if the private actor is a "willful participant in joint activity with the State or its agents" (*Lugar v. Edmonson Oil Company*, 1982, pp. 937, 941).

NEW DIRECTIONS FOR INSTITUTIONAL RESEARCH • DOI: 10.1002/ir

Following this trilogy, most courts have declined to find state action for accreditors (e.g., *McKeesport Hospital v. ACGME*, 1994; *NCAA v. Tarkanian*, 1988). More recently, however, the Supreme Court held in *Brentwood Academy* (2001) that a secondary school accrediting agency was a state actor. Brentwood Academy, a private high school, sought to prevent the Association from enforcing a rule prohibiting the use of undue influence in student athlete recruiting efforts. The Court explained that prior cases had "tr[ied] to plot a line between state action subject to Fourteenth Amendment scrutiny and private conduct (however exceptionable) that is not," and aimed not to impose responsibility on the State for conduct beyond its control, but rather to assure constitutional protections when the State is responsible for the conduct (p. 930). Said the Court, state action "may be found if, though only if, there is such a 'close nexus between the State and the challenged action' that seemingly private behavior 'may be fairly treated as that of the State itself'" (*Brentwood Academy*, 2001, p. 930).

The *Brentwood Academy* (2001) Court clarified that "the character of a legal entity is determined neither by its expressly private characterization in statutory law, nor by the failure of the law to acknowledge the entity's inseparability from recognized government officials or agencies" (*Brentwood Academy*, 2001, p. 931). Notably, the Court explained that "[t]he nominally private character of the Association is overborne by the pervasive entwinement of public institutions and public officials in its composition and workings ..." (*Brentwood Academy*, 2001, p. 932). The Association was comprised primarily of public schools; its controlling members were predominantly public school officials who were eligible for membership in the state retirement system. Based on "entwinement," the Court judged the Association's actions by constitutional standards (*Brentwood Academy*, 2001, p. 933).

The *Auburn University* (2002) Court subsequently questioned whether the entwinement theory would alter interpretations of state action cases. Although accreditation had not been considered a public function, the 1992 amendments to the HEA more closely linked the Secretary of Education and the accrediting agencies' actions. The Secretary's recognition was based on its review of the agency, from criteria to operations procedures. Said the court:

> It may be that the Court's "pervasive entwinement" theory articulated in *Brentwood Academy* will supersede the legal fiction of courts denying that accrediting agencies are state actors, but declaring them to be "quasi-public" organizations bound by "common law due process." (*Auburn University*, 2002, p. 1373)

Additional Factors Showing Entwinement. Although accrediting activities are deemed voluntary, are conducted by peers, and have some standards set by the agencies themselves, extensive parameters for accreditors' actions are dictated by the Secretary of Education and by Congress through the HEA. Quality, for example, is influenced by myriad "areas" such as "[f]iscal and administrative capacity" as may be appropriate to an individual institution's operations (34 C.F.R. § 602.16(1)(v), 2015). Additionally, the Secretary dictates how an agency must enforce its own standards (34 C.F.R. § 602.20, 2015) and ensure due process is met (34 C.F.R. § 602.25, 2015). The federal government further dictates processes an accreditor must take if an institution is not in compliance with a particular standard (34 C.F.R. § 602.20, 2015).

The HEA grants exclusive jurisdiction to United States district courts for educational institutions that challenge the "denial, withdrawal, or termination of accreditation" (20 U.S.C. § 1099b(f), 2012). Section 1099b(f) gives federal courts exclusive jurisdiction over disputes involving accreditation, resolving such disputes through a common law claim for due process and adequate judicial review. A grant of federal jurisdiction occurs when there is a comprehensive regulatory scheme (*Massachusetts School of Law*, 1998). Deeming accreditation an "important national function," the *Massachusetts School of Law* court explained, "[t]he Higher Education Act and the DOE's implementing regulations spin a sophisticated regulatory web governing the relationship between accrediting agencies and accreditation applicants" (1998, p. 33).

Although the *Professional Massage* (2015) Court described agency-like standards and deemed administrative law "useful in determining the standard by which [to] review the agency's decisionmaking process," (p. 171) it would not "go so far as to say the [accreditor] is equivalent to a federal agency" bound by the Administrative Procedures Act (pp. 170). Even so, the court deemed deference appropriate and compared the accreditation agency's expertise and knowledge to that of federal administrative agency expertise.

Conclusions

A binding thread runs through historical and legal accounts of higher education accreditation: Accreditation's purpose was and is to protect the public. Since the earliest formation of the accreditation system, the federal government has not directly accredited institutions of higher education. Even so, the history and case law elucidate that notions of voluntary participation by institutions and labels of private applied to accrediting agencies are becoming increasingly obsolete with each iteration of laws imposed on the relationship between the federal government, accreditors, and institutions.

If faced with a potentially adverse accreditation decision, IR practitioners may find both solace and frustration that there is no litmus test against which to judge. Leaders choosing to fight adverse accrediting actions should prepare for a fact-intensive inquiry, primarily focusing on accessing and re-

New Directions for Institutional Research • DOI: 10.1002/ir

sponding to detailed agency rules and regulations and determining whether the agency's policies and procedures were fairly applied. Because the superficial line of demarcation in the public/private dichotomy is ever shifting towards accreditors' public status—increasing the alignment with state action jurisprudence—any challenge to an adverse accreditation decision warrants consideration of claims of common law *and* constitutional protections.

References

Alstete, J. W. (2007). *College accreditation: Managing internal revitalization and public respect.* New York, NY: Palgrave Macmillan.

Auburn University v. Southern Association of Colleges & Schools, Inc., 489 F. Supp. 2d 1362 (N.D. Ga. 2002).

Bloand, H. G. (2001). *Creating the Council for Higher Education Accreditation (CHEA).* Phoenix, AZ: The Oryx Press.

Blum v. Yaretsky, 457 U.S. 991 (1982).

Brentwood Academy v. Tennessee Secondary School Athletic Association, 531 U.S. 288 (2001).

Capone, L. III. (2009). *Accreditation: What the general counsel needs to know; A focus on due process challenges to adverse accreditation actions.* Washington, DC: The National Association of College and University Attorneys, 1–14. Retrieved from http://www-local.legal.uillinois.edu/nacua09/Disk2/presentations/4C_Handout.pdf

Chicago School of Automatic Transmissions, Inc. v. Accreditation Alliance of Career Schools & Colleges, 44 F.3d 447 (7th Cir. 1994).

Cohen, A. M., & Kisker, C. B. (2010). The shaping of American higher education: Emergence and growth of the contemporary system. San Francisco, CA: Jossey-Bass.

Edward Waters College, Inc. v. Southern Association of Colleges & Schools, Inc., 2005 WL 6218035, No. 3:05-cv-180J-16HTS (M.D.Fla. 11 March 2005).

Flood, J. T., & Dewhirst, D. (2014). Shedding the shibboleth: Judicial acknowledgement that higher education accreditors are state actors. *The Georgetown Journal of Law and Public Policy, 12,* 731–784.

Fuller, M. B. (2014). A history of financial aid to students. *Journal of Student Financial Aid, 44*(1), 42-68.

Fuller, M. B., & Lugg, E. T. (2012). Legal precedents for higher education accreditation. *The Journal of Higher Education Management, 27*(1), 47–88.

Gaston, P. L. (2014). *Higher education accreditation: How it's changing, why it must.* Sterling, VA: Stylus.

Higher Education Act of 1965,Pub. L. No. 89-329, 79 Stat. 1219 (current version at 20 U.S.C. §§ 1001 to 1161aa-1).

Jeffries v. Georgia Residential Finance Authority, 678 F.2d 919, 922 (11th Cir. 1982).

Kaplin, W. A. (1969). Judicial review of accreditation: The *Parsons College* case. *The Journal of Higher Education 40,* 543–554.

Leas, T. (1991). Higher education, the courts, and the "doctrine" of academic abstention. *The Journal of Law and Education, 20,* 135–165.

Lubinescu, E. S., Ratcliff, J. L., & Gaffney, M. A. (2001). Two continuums collide: Accreditation and assessment. *New Directions for Higher Education, 113,* 5–21.

Lugar v. Edmonson Oil Company, 457 U.S. 992 (1982).

Marjorie Webster Junior College, Inc. v. Middle States Association of Colleges & Secondary Schools, Inc., 302 F. Supp. 455 (D.D.C. 1969), *rev'd,* 432 F.2d 650 (D.C. Cir. 1970).

Massachusetts School of Law at Andover, Inc. v. American Bar Association, 142 F.3d 26 (1st Cir. 1998).

McKeesport Hospital v. Accreditation Council for Graduate Medical Education, 24 F.3d 519 (3d Cir. 1994).

Medical Institute of Minnesota v. National Association of Trade & Technical Schools, 817 F.2d 1310 (8th Cir. 1987).

Molinero, S. (2013). Reexamining the examiners: The need for increased government regulation of accreditation in higher education. *Duquesne L. R.*, *51*, 833–858.

National Collegiate Athletic Association v. Tarkanian, 488 U.S. 179 (1988).

National Defense Education Act of 1958, Pub. L. No. 85-864, 72 Stat. 1580 (current version at 20 USC 17 §§ 401*et seq*).

North Dakota v. North Central Association of Colleges & Secondary Schools, 23 F. Supp. 694 (E.D. Ill. 1938), aff'd, 99 F.2d 697 (7th Cir. 1938).

Parsons College v. North Central Association of Colleges & Secondary Schools, 271 F. Supp. 65 (N.D. Ill. 1967).

Professional Massage Training Center, Inc. v. Accreditation Alliance of Career Schools & Colleges, 781 F.3d 161 (4th Cir. 2015).

Rendell-Baker v. Kohn, 57 U.S. 830 (1982).

Rockland Institute, Division of Amistad Vocational Schools, Inc. v. Association of Independent Colleges & Schools, 412 F. Supp. 1015 (C. D. Cal. 1976).

Scalia, A. (1989). Judicial deference to administrative interpretations of law. *Duke Law Journal*, *1989*(3), 511–521.

Servicemen's Readjustment Act of 1944 (G.I. Bill), Pub. L. No. 78-346, 58 Stat. 284.

Sherman Antitrust Act of 1890, 15 USC §§ 1–7 (2012).

Sojourner-Douglass College v. Middle States Association of Colleges and Schools, 2015 WL 5091994 (D. Md. August 27, 2015).

St. Agnes Hospital of the City of Baltimore, Inc. v. Riddick (I), 668 F. Supp. 478 (D. Md. 1987).

Synder, T. (1993). *120 years of American education: A statistical portrait*. Washington, DC: National Center for Education Statistics.

Thelin, J. R. (2011). *A history of American higher education*. (2nd ed.). Baltimore, MD: The Johns Hopkins University Press.

Thomas M. Cooley Law School v. American Bar Association, 459 F.3d 705 (6th Cir. 2006), cert. denied, 549 U.S. 1116 (2007).

U.S. Department of Veterans Affairs. (2016). *Education and training: History and timeline*. Retrieved from http://www.benefits.va.gov/gibill/history.asp

Vanderbilt University. (2015a). *The cost of federal regulatory compliance in higher education: A multi-institutional study*. Retrieved from http://news.vanderbilt. edu/files/Regulatory-Compliance-Report-Final.pdf

Vanderbilt University. (2015b). *The cost of federal regulatory compliance at Vanderbilt University*. Retrieved from http://news.vanderbilt.edu/files/2015-VU-CRC-Summary.pdf

Veterans' Readjustment Act of 1952, Pub. L. No. 82-550, 66 Stat. 663.

Wheelan, B. S., & Elgart, M. A. (2015, October). Accreditation's real cost (and value). *Inside Higher Ed*. Retrieved from https://www.insidehighered.com/views/2015/10/22/real-costs-accreditation-and-processs-value-essay

20 U.S.C. § 1099b(f) (2012).

34 C.F.R. § 602.16(1)(v) (2015).

34 C.F.R. § 602.20 (2015).

34 C.F.R. § 602.25 (2015).

JULEE T. FLOOD, JD, PhD, Fellow, Elon University School of Law.

JEFF ROBERTS, MA, Director of Assessment, Sam Houston State University.

This chapter asserts that the use and reporting of institutional research (IR) data is an area ripe for litigation. The chapter explores possible student causes of action as they relate to institutional research (IR) data and compares the probable outcomes to reported student lawsuits. The chapter concludes with recommended liability-avoiding practices for IR offices.

When Does Institutional Research Rhetoric Create a Student Cause of Action?

Rhonda Vickers Beassie, JD

Institutions frequently collect information with the goal of benchmarking current conditions, altering materials, programs, and processes and then gathering follow-up data to demonstrate a change. Colleges and universities conduct assessments of programs and educational activities expecting to demonstrate improvement in educational outcomes. The institution may conduct surveys and promote participation through publicity, policies, and incentives that communicate a particular course, program, or even the experience of an entire student body is now improved. Yet, what is the recourse for students when such proclamations are premature, incomplete, inaccurate, or ultimately unfounded? Did the institution's assessment rhetoric create a legally actionable promise, or even a duty, to students? When does the marketing of the labors of institutional research (IR) intersect with a potential litigant's cause of action?

Institutions are more likely to be sued by students today than ever before (Lake, 2009). In the litigious American culture, one can reasonably expect an attorney to fashion a claim for a student or alumnus based upon an institution's lack of pledged progress. However, as detailed below, proving liability and securing a judgment is much more challenging. Student-initiated litigation centered on education claims primarily includes allegations of broken promises, misrepresentation, or breach of obligations. Given the difficulty of substantiating these claims, such suits are rarely successful and while an institution may be required to defend its assessment practices, data, or reports, it is unlikely, under present jurisprudence, that legal liability will follow.

In view of the limited potential of losing a lawsuit, why would an institution invest time in shaping assessment processes and related

NEW DIRECTIONS FOR INSTITUTIONAL RESEARCH, no. 172 © 2017 Wiley Periodicals, Inc.
Published online in Wiley Online Library (wileyonlinelibrary.com) • DOI: 10.1002/ir.20206

communications with an eye towards avoiding legal exposure? Because institutions have an interest in avoiding the high cost of defending litigation. As recently as 2013, the National Center for State Courts, Court Statistics Project estimated the median direct costs of a typical contract lawsuit, a common student cause of action, at $91,000 (Hannaford-Agor & Waters, 2013, p. 6). This estimate demonstrates easily quantifiable legal expenses such as attorney's fees, but does not include the significant indirect costs of responsive personnel time and damage to an institution's reputation. To help prevent or minimize lawsuits or aid in ending legal action early, institutions should take time to review assessment practices and communications that may give rise to a claim that the institution breached a promise or duty to its students. The rhetoric and commentary of assessment—how program goals, anticipated results, or interpretation of actual data are used and referenced in speeches, reports, or websites—is possible evidence for litigants seeking remedies for an unmet promise or duty.

This chapter reviews cases where students accuse their college or university of failing to make good on a promise or representation related to academics or academic support programs. Beginning with analysis of tort-based claims, the most common student causes of action against educational institutions, educational malpractice and misrepresentation are explored. As most publicly available institutional publications are deemed a contract between the student and school, examination of possible breach of contract cases are explored. The final student lawsuits considered are the consumer-oriented statutory claims of recent law students regarding institutional collection and publication of employment statistics. Personal injury and discrimination claims are less likely to have a connection to assessment, thus are beyond the scope of analysis in the present chapter. The discussion concludes with practice recommendations for IR offices.

In each case discussed below, the student asserts he or she believed attending the school, participating in the program, or taking the course of action advocated by the institution would result in a furtherance or upgrade of his or her education or employment prospects. When the expected outcome did not occur, the student sued. Student-centered assessment processes, including course-level placement, employment statistics, faculty evaluations, and satisfaction or engagement surveys may provide documentation of an institutional obligation or promise to students. The most common causes of action for student plaintiffs are breach of contract, claims under consumer protection or deceptive trade statute, or torts.

Torts

Tort claims may fragment into a variety of claims; however, in the simplest form a tort is an intentional or negligent wrongful act or omission that harms another. To be legally actionable, the wrongdoer or tortfeasor, must have a duty to the plaintiff. One has a duty when (1) the relationship between the parties create a responsibility (e.g., childcare provider and child), (2) a statute dictates a duty (e.g., environmental protection requirements for landowners), (3) the closeness or proximity of the parties creates the obligation (e.g., you cannot drive into a lane occupied by another), or (4) the harm is foreseeable and a reasonable person would find it fair and reasonable that a duty exists. The threshold for bringing a tort action is demonstrating that the wrongdoer owed a duty of care, he or she breached the duty, and the plaintiff suffered harm as a result or cause of the breach (Tokic, 2014). To transition from a physical injury example to the education context, consider student tortious claims of educational malpractice and misrepresentation.

Educational Malpractice

As early as the 1970s, plaintiffs asserted academic institutions had a legal duty for the provision or quality of education and education related services and liability for the breach or failure of a duty (*Peter W. v. San Francisco Unified Sch. Dist.*, 1976). Since then, federal and state courts routinely, and almost uniformly, deny this avenue of litigation and do not recognize educational malpractice as a legitimate cause of action (Beh, 2000).

Failure to Teach Necessary Subject and Public Policy: Moore v. Vanderloo.   In 1986, the Supreme Court of Iowa, considered the tort of educational malpractice in *Moore v. Vanderloo* (1986). Moore suffered a stroke after receiving chiropractic care from Vanderloo. Among other defendants, she sued the chiropractor and Palmer College of Chiropractic where Vanderloo had earned his degree four years earlier. Moore claimed the chiropractic college failed to teach Vanderloo certain risks of stroke. The court deemed the case against the college to be a claim for educational malpractice.

After reviewing decisions from other jurisdictions, the court articulated five public policy reasons for declining to recognize the tort, specifically:

1. In education, each institution, indeed, each instructor, has a degree of independence to determine classroom approach and level of emphasis placed on specific topics within a broad subject matter. There is therefore no industry standard for teaching or selection/creation of curriculum for a court to compare against a plaintiff's claims.
2. Educational injuries are difficult to define. Many variables, including student intellectual capacity, prior educational preparation, class attendance, and time devoted to studies are too far beyond the institution's control to establish the necessary causation element of a tort claim.
3. If permitted, educational malpractice claims are likely to increase litigation, create a significant burden for schools, and increase costs for both educational consumers and taxpayers.

4. Education based torts threaten the judiciary's long history of deferring and declining to interfere in institutions of higher education policies, governance, management and academic freedom.
5. Many educational programs and the professions students enter following graduation are highly regulated by other bodies such as legislatures or professional boards (Vanderloo, 1986, pp. 114–116) . Other jurisdictions considering educational malpractice claims often echo the Vanderloo rationales and, invariably deny redress under that theory.

Negligence in Instruction: *Miller v. Loyola University of New Orleans*.   Even with clear and repeated reasons for rejecting educational malpractice, students, whether through genuine frustration or simply searching for a big payoff, continue to file lawsuits. As demonstrated in Vanderloo, when student plaintiffs avoid using the word "malpractice," courts are, nevertheless, likely to dispose of an assertion of academic wrongdoing by couching the claim as educational malpractice. The Forth Circuit Court of Appeal of Louisiana did so in *Miller v. Loyola University of New Orleans* (2002). Miller, a student plaintiff, sought damages for a claim that Loyola breached the duty of appropriately delivering a required course (2002, p. 1059). Prior to initiating the lawsuit, Miller made his complaints known to the school. The administration investigated and found many of Miller's complaints regarding the quality of instruction and insufficient coverage of necessary topics had merit. Loyola's response was to sanction the professor and offer affected students the opportunity to audit the class at no cost. Miller did not accept the school's offer and instead elected to pay and enroll in the course a second time with a different instructor. He later filed a lawsuit asserting several claims, including negligence in providing education and selecting faculty (Miller, 2002, p. 1059).

The Louisiana Court of Appeal did not consider whether the plaintiff met the elements of duty, breach, cause, and damage described above. Instead, the court determined that the basis for Miller's lawsuit—his cause of action—was centered on the quality of education and was therefore one of educational malpractice. As Louisiana courts had not previously decided an educational malpractice case, the court reviewed cases from other jurisdictions and in extending the logic of those decisions, found that Miller failed to state a valid cause of action (2002, p. 1060). The court determined "Universities must be allowed the flexibility to manage themselves and correct their own mistakes" (Miller 2002, p. 1061). Loyola had done just that by considering Miller's complaint, taking administrative action to investigate, and offering the plaintiff the remedy of auditing the course at no cost. As such, the court declined to evaluate or interfere in the institution's management of the situation (Miller, 2002).

In Miller, we see that even when an institution admits inadequacy in the education provided, courts remain loath to find a breach of duty. Such

NEW DIRECTIONS FOR INSTITUTIONAL RESEARCH • DOI: 10.1002/ir

decisions may give IR staff a level of comfort and confidence in collecting data, especially when data may reveal unfavorable information. However, it is worth noting that the court in Miller resisted evaluating Loyola's academic decisions, at least in part, because the school conducted an independent review and instituted corrective measures addressing the deficiency. Likewise, institutions should have procedures in place to evaluate information collected, address shortcomings, and document responses. This is as true for material assembled in response to an internal investigation as in the Miller case, as for information compiled as part of an assessment process.

Misrepresentation

Misrepresentation claims usually involve an allegation that an institution supplied false or misleading information regarding a material issue, the student acted in reliance upon the information provided, and suffered harm as a result (Taylor, 2015). When a litigant demonstrates false or misleading information was knowingly, intentionally, and specifically provided, the cause of action may be fraud, fraudulent misrepresentation, or intentional misrepresentation. When there was no purposeful communication of misinformation specifically provided to a student, the action is likely labeled negligent misrepresentation. Institutions are seldom liable for education related torts of fraudulent or negligent misrepresentation (Taylor, 2015). However, the exception to this rule was reviewed in *Sain v. Cedar Rapids Community School District* (2001).

Negligent Misrepresentation: *Sain v. Cedar Rapids Community School District*.   While an all-state high school basketball player in Cedar Rapids, Sain, sought assistance from his guidance counselor when selecting an English course. Allegedly, the counselor advised that a Technical Communications course would fulfill the NCAA core English course requirement. Relying upon the counselor's statements, Sain enrolled and completed the course. During that same trimester, Northern Illinois University awarded Sain a full, 5-year basketball scholarship. However, after graduation, the NCAA informed Sain that his Technical Communications course was not accepted and he was therefore ineligible to play. This course deficiency resulted in the loss of scholarship and without financial assistance Sain was unable to attend Northern Illinois University. He sued the school district, claiming negligence and negligent misrepresentation.

The trial court dismissed the case, and Sain appealed to the Supreme Court of Iowa. To prevent the injustice, the court determined that the facts of each education-related claim must be weighed against the public policy arguments for limiting educational malpractice articulated in *Vanderloo* (*Sain*, 2001). The appellate court concluded it could analyze and make a decision upon the alleged misrepresentation without interfering in Cedar Rapids' educational operations or touching upon any of the other Vanderloo public policy concerns.

NEW DIRECTIONS FOR INSTITUTIONAL RESEARCH • DOI: 10.1002/ir

Per the court, school counselors serve in an advisory capacity by supplying information educational institutions expect students to rely upon. As such, counselors are professionals, owing a duty of reasonable care to the individuals directly receiving their information or advice (*Sain*, 2001, p. 124, citing and applying the Restatement (Second of Torts) § 552(1)). When a school counselor fails in that duty, there is potential liability for damages caused by the breach (*Sain*, 2001). The court reversed the dismissal and returned Sain's case to the trial court. Although he won at the appellate level, the amount of damages ultimately recovered are unknown, as he settled with the Cedar Rapids Community School District before trial (Stone, 2006). Although Sain's claims arose in a high school counseling context, the court's analysis of institutional liability for misinformation is instructive for higher education leaders. The decision carefully limited negligent misrepresentation to circumstances where the intended recipient directly received information from a professional and suffered harm because of reasonable reliance on the guidance. Even though IR staff rarely engage in the type of direct communication with students or members of the public contemplated by the *Sain* court, reliance on distributed assessment or course catalog data, which many IR staff do oversee, can form the basis of consumer-based liability claims.

This review of student tort claims demonstrates the dynamic nature of the law. With a reasoned analysis of judicial decisions from several jurisdictions, the Supreme Court of Iowa carefully considered, and then artfully discarded, educational malpractice as a recognized cause of action, even when the plaintiff demonstrated permanent physical injury as the harm (*Vanderloo*, 1986). Yet, just 15 years later, the same court distinguished its earlier decision and determined an educational institution could, in fact, be liable for breaching a duty of care when a guidance counselor provides misinformation (*Sain*, 2001). Currently, the potential legal liability for institutional assessment is limited. However, institutional tortuous liability has, and shall continue, to evolve. Data, reports, statements, and even research processes that appear innocuous today may very well be the basis of, or evidence for, a lawsuit tomorrow.

Breach of Contract

While few courts acknowledge a duty of care between an institution of higher education and its students, many recognize contractual relationship (Beh, 2000). To demonstrate a cause of action in contract, a student must show only the existence of a valid contract and damage resulting from an institution's violation of the agreement. Although not negotiated or expressly executed, most courts find students of higher education institutions enter into an implied agreement (*Andre v. Pace University*, 1996; *Ross v. Creighton University*, 1992). Implied contracts are those that, while perhaps not clearly defined in writing and signed by both parties, are inferred by the conduct of the parties. Such agreements are enforceable promises (Restatement, 1981). Institution policies, catalogues, brochures, websites, and, potentially, assessment reports provide the terms of the implied contract and thus, the burden is on the student plaintiff to establish that the college or university breached an obligation.

Breach of Procedure Detailed in Catalogue: *Supplee v. Miller-Motte Business College.* In a recent student lawsuit, the college catalogue was deemed evidence of a contractual obligation (*Supplee v. Miller-Motte Business College*, 2015). Supplee claimed breach of contract, along with tort and statutory claims against his former institution, Miller-Motte Business College. The Miller-Motte catalogue stated the college would check the criminal history of applicants and review any reported convictions when determining a student's admission eligibility. The college admitted Supplee and after a year of enrollment finally completed his background check. Upon review of his criminal history, Supplee was advised that he could not fulfill the requirements of the program (2015). At trial, the jury found for Supplee on the theory that the college breached the student/institution contract and the court ordered Miller-Motte to pay damages of over $50,000. The college argued that review of Supplee's claim would require judicial inquiry into the academic freedom and educational operations of the college. However, the appellate court deemed the background check requirement a specifically identified contractual obligation that did not require interference with academic decisions or process. Further, the background requirement was a significant institutional obligation because the results could preclude admission and thereby defeat the entire agreement. The North Carolina Court of Appeals found the college's failure to secure Supplee's background check was a material breach of contract and upheld the trial court judgment against Miller-Motte (2015).

Breach of Course Level Categorization in Catalogue: *Andre v. Pace University.* By contrast, the judgment awarding two computer-programming students a refund of tuition for breach of contract and other claims was overturned on appeal in *Andre v. Pace University* (1996). Per the students, the institution breached the contract when failing to deliver a "basic" course (as described in the catalogue) at the appropriate instructional level (*Andre*, 1996, pp. 778–779). Prior to enrolling in the basic graduate-level programming course, students Andre and Broom met with the department chair to discuss their prior education and whether their limited mathematics experience was sufficient for performance in a beginning programming class. From the text of the decision, it does not appear that the institution required, or offered, placement assessment testing to the students. Instead, the chair merely voiced encouraging assurances and the students enrolled. They shortly experienced difficulty, withdrew, and requested a refund. When Pace offered only a tuition credit, Andre and Broom sued and won at trial (*Andre*, p. 778).

NEW DIRECTIONS FOR INSTITUTIONAL RESEARCH • DOI: 10.1002/ir

However, the university appealed and the New York appellate court found that even though the students and the school had a contractual relationship, promises related to quality or process of instruction are not appropriate for judicial review (*Andre*, 1996, p. 779). The chair's advice to the students regarding their preparedness for course was, according to the appellate court, merely an individual opinion and not an actionable contractual promise (*Andre*, 1996, p. 780). Evaluation of the plaintiff's allegations of inappropriate course description or instruction would necessitate investigation into the university's curriculum choices and teaching methods. The court therefore considered the plaintiff's claims tantamount to an educational malpractice cause of action. As educational malpractice is not recognized in New York, the appellate court found the trial court erred by interfering in Pace University's educational decisions (*Andre*, 1996, p. 780).

Taken in tandem, the cases against Miller-Motte and Pace demonstrate the contractual nature of institutional communications and how costly even a single word can be to a school. Note that although Pace University ultimately won, the expense of defending the lawsuit surely outweighed the tuition and fees generated from Andre and Broom. Various forms of institutional and assessment data are published and/or available to the university community and beyond the walls of the institution. When the data or information is located where a student may review and reasonably rely on the statement, it is a potential contract and should be treated as such.

Consider, for example, an isolated assessment indicator published such as "studies show student satisfaction with X University has increased 35 percent in the last five years." Although there is much to question about this statement, such a generalized and promotional assertion likely lacks the specificity necessary for a contractual obligation. Thus, unless analysis of the referenced study data was in error, or simply falsified, this communication could not be evidence of a breach of failing to continue to improve in student satisfaction.

However, consider the potential liability created by a website or brochure containing a mixture of research results and related plans, such as "The department has undergone a program-wide curricular review and announces improved instruction based upon evidence-based assessment." Such statements are commonplace in today's market-driven economy and in college or university accountability reports. Assume a former student, one experienced with previous departmental teaching methods, enrolls in classes because of the announcement. During the semester, it becomes apparent to the student that nothing in the instruction has changed; hence, it has not improved. Indeed, when the student asks the faculty members how teaching changed after the program-wide review, it is clear there is no instructor commitment to the announced improvements. Armed with this information, the student believes the institution failed to deliver on a promise and his time and tuition constitute damages. He or she may be successful in demonstrating the elements necessary to file a breach of contract claim.

This scenario, coupled with the cases above, demonstrate that communication of the data collected and analyzed by IR staff can connect to contract-based claims, even when merely extrapolated into an aspirational statement. A court may ultimately deem the departmental improvement announcement to be mere nonactionable puffery or too vague to be a term of contract (Taylor, 2015). Further, like the decision in Andre, a court may decline to evaluate the touted curricular and teaching improvements and dismiss this hypothetical contract claim. Regardless, the institution may have invested time and resources in defending a carelessly worded goal based upon data maintained and/or reported by the institution (and in some cases specifically by IR).

Statutory Claims

Statutory claims against institutions are generally a variation of the misrepresentation, fraud, and contract causes of action discussed above. The difference is a legislatively enacted mandate—most commonly state consumer protection statutes—to detail the inappropriate institutional action and available remedy. In such cases, the student plaintiff asserts that the institution made statements misrepresenting material facts about the program and in so doing, the school engaged in deceptive trade practices.

Since 2010, the most newsworthy statutory claims are law school cases where students claim the reported graduate employment information was unfair, misleading, fraudulent, and/or deceptive (Eckman, 2012). While some included claims based in contract or tort theories, the primary cause of action for law school employment litigation was consumer protection or deceptive trade statutes (*Alaburda v. Thomas Jefferson School of Law*, 2011; *Casey v. Florida Coastal School of Law*, 2015; Eckman, 2012; *Gomez-Jimenez v. New York Law School*, December 20, 2012; *Harnish v. Widener University School of Law*, 2013; *MacDonald v. Thomas M. Cooley Law School*, 2012). In these cases, a student, alumni, or group of alumni claimed the law school published employment information on websites or in marketing materials that materially misrepresented the actual information the student relied upon when deciding to attend the school. The cost of 3 years of legal education generally exceeds $100,000 (*MacDonald,* 2012). Basing their harm on their law school expenses, the unemployed or under-employed law graduates claimed serious dollar value damages.

The law school accrediting body, the American Bar Association (ABA) requires an annual accounting of the employment of every single law graduate at the time of graduation and again 9 months after graduation. In addition to compulsory reporting, law schools send employment information to various organizations and publications. Law schools are under significant pressure to account for jobs. With such attention on this one measure, one assumes a law school would entrust this function to the professional research arm of the institution.

However, according to the plaintiffs, collection efforts and data analysis was deficient and communication of the data lacked integrity. The legal employment statistics were often compiled by laypersons with no research or statistical experience. According to testimony in one case, the alumni relations office compiled and reported the employment data (Bennion, 2016). The lawsuits claimed gross employment figures were reported on websites and in marketing material, which included nonlegal employment, part-time jobs, school-funded internships, and self-employment (Casey, 2015, p. 4). Allegedly, even a barista position counted as law graduate employment at New York Law School (*Gomez-Jimenez v. New York Law School*, March 21, 2012, p. 839). Moreover, some schools asserted average starting salaries for an entire graduating class based on only a very small number of survey respondents, in some cases as low as 20% of the graduates (*Gomez-Jimenez*, March 21, 2012, p. 845).

Most courts found that the law schools were following the guidelines provided by the accrediting body and that re-reporting of this information was not technically inaccurate or false. As the employment figures were not complete fabrications, for the statutory claims to survive, the litigants were required to prove reasonable reliance upon the deceptive statements. Law alumni plaintiffs have largely been unable to meet this burden. Prospective law students are educated and sophisticated consumers (*MacDonald*, 2012). As such, courts indicated plaintiffs were obligated to evaluate the legal employment market instead of solely relying upon the self-serving reports and statements of the schools. In making these findings, courts were persuaded by the education and knowledge of prospective law students, the responsibility a consumer has when making a significant purchase such as a law degree, and the massive legal layoffs the market was experiencing at the time most students were selecting law schools in 2008 (*Casey*, 2015, *Gomez-Jimenez*, March 21, 2012). Even when the *MacDonald* judge determined the school's reported employment figures were "inconsistent, confusing, and inherently untrustworthy" (*MacDonald*, 2012, p. 15) the court declined to extend consumer protection laws intended for personal transactions to the purchase of a legal education. To date, all statutory and other claims related to assessment and reporting of law school employment failed.

It is likely that the law graduates were unsuccessful with statutory claims, at least in part, because underemployed lawyers make unsympathetic plaintiffs. The outcome of a lawsuit with a less sophisticated and more likable prospective student relying on equally sloppy or distorted reported research when selecting a school, a major, or even participating in a costly study abroad might very well be different (Lake, 2009).

In addition to the concern of lawsuits brought by individual students or a class of students, federal and state government is increasingly active in pursuing statutory claims against higher education institutions publishing

NEW DIRECTIONS FOR INSTITUTIONAL RESEARCH • DOI: 10.1002/ir

misleading information. To date, the targets have principally been for-profit institutions, such as the False Claims Act suit/settlement with Education Management Corporation and the Federal Trade Commission Act claim against DeVry University (Smith, 2016; Stratford, 2015). Currently, public policy arguments appear to preclude governmental action against public and nonprofit institutions; however, the door to such action is now open.

Practice Recommendations for IR Staff

Armed with an understanding that IR operations can form the basis of a claim or evidence for litigation, IR offices can protect the organization by putting procedures under the microscope. Two areas ripe for legal claims are data publication and retention.

Publication.   Researchers do not always have knowledge of the ultimate use of data and may be unaware of the ultimate audience that will receive, review, and rely upon reported results that can give rise to contractual or misrepresentation claims. Occasionally, institutions put pressure on IR staff to release data not yet vetted for factual accuracy or full statistical validity. Later, IR staff may find the partial information broadcast with an inaccurate interpretation or inappropriate extrapolation to unrelated facts or scenarios. Worse, even well-intentioned administrators sometimes seek modification, particularly of statistical information with or without the complicity of IR offices.

To guard against incomplete and inaccurate reporting and in managing organizational legal risks, IR offices should consider limiting the release and use of institutional data. Such protocols may include a description of the parameters of the data collection and limited reach of the analysis. IR offices might even add a disclaimer to this description prior to distributing information. Further, IR staff can be assigned as department liaisons and preprint reviewers of any publications that include references to assessment results. Before green-lighting print, IR staff should verify the accuracy of statements related to IR data and ensure removal of promissory language such as "students taking x class/program *will* perform better," or "our commitment to you."

Limit Unnecessary Data.   The best litigation shield is to avoid collection and retention of unnecessary data. Arguably, if there is no plan to evaluate or use data, the information should neither be collected, nor maintained. After all, even in the infancy of widespread educational assessment departments, the American Association of Higher Education Principles of Good Practice asserted that research should be based upon a specific question with advance consideration of how and by whom the information will be used (Hutchings, Ewell, & Banta, 2013).

IR staff may have many counter arguments for limiting collection and retention data such as increasing accreditation and accountability requirements. The changing education landscape makes it tempting, and indeed it may have become an industry standard, to store all available information in the event it may, one day, prove to be valuable for an unidentified future research project. However, institutions warehousing expired or unanalyzed information are more likely expending valuable resources by accumulating and maintaining discoverable evidence for use by the next plaintiff bringing a cause of action against the school.

Conclusion

Given the resistance of courts to claims from college and university students, the potential liability for assessment-related litigation is, at present, fairly low. However, even in the face of almost uniform rejection of cases claiming institutional educational deficiencies, litigants continue to claim harm and the lawsuits keep coming. We are in an age where students approach education with a consumerism mentality and an age of increased governmental measurement and accountability. As such, we may see a continued chipping away at judicial resistance to addressing student claims, including promises relating to instructional quality, against education institutions. When that day comes, assessment practices, claims, data, and promises will be highly scrutinized in determining liability for schools that fail to meet stated goals or fulfill promises made in reports and recruiting literature. IR staff can prepare for this eventuality by examining and refining protocols to verify accuracy of research results reported, review of non-department assessment-related publications, and limiting the volume of data collected and maintained.

References

Alaburda, v. Thomas Jefferson School of Law, 2012 WL 6039151 (Cal. Super. Ct. Trial Div. 2012).

Andre v. Pace University, 655 N.Y.S.2d 777 (1996).

Beh, G. H. (2000). Student versus university: The university's implied obligations of good faith and fair dealing. *59 Md. L. Rev.*, 183–224.

Bennion, J. (2016). Understanding the Alaburda v. Thomas Jefferson law verdict. *Above the Law*. Retrieved fromhttp://abovethelaw.com/2016/03/understanding-the-alaburda-v-thomas-jefferson-law-verdict-a-conversation-with-one-of-the-jurors/ATL_understanding-the-alaburda-v-TJSL

Casey v. Florida Coastal School of Law, Inc., 2015 WL 10096085 (M.D. Florida 2015).

Eckman, D. (2012). Rethinking lawsuits against law schools: Graduates must overcome significant hurdles. *Journal of Law & Education*, 42 (Summer 2013), 575–583.

Gomez-Jimenez v. New York Law School, 943 N.Y.S.2d 834 (March 21, 2012).

Gomez-Jimenez v. New York Law School, 103 A.D.3d 13 (December 20, 2012).

Hannaford-Agor, P., & Waters N. L. (2013, January). Estimating the cost of civil litigation. *Court Statistics Project*, 20(1).

Harnish v. Widener University School of Law, 2013 WL 1890276 (2013).

Hutchings, P., Ewell, P., & Banta, T. (2013). AAHE principles of good practice: Aging nicely. Champaign, IL: National Institute for Learning Outcomes

Assessment. Retrieved from http://www.learningoutcomesassessment.org/Principles ofAssessment.html

Lake, P. F. (2009, August 11). Will your college be sued for educational malpractice? *The Chronicle of Higher Education.* Retrievedfrom http://chronicle.com/ article/Educational-Malpractice-/47980/

MacDonald v. Thomas M. Cooley Law School, 880 F. Supp.2d 785 (2012).

Miller v. Loyola University of New Orleans, 829 So.2d 1057 (2002).

Moore v. Vanderloo, 386 N.W.2d 108 (1986).

Peter W. v. San Francisco Unified School District, 60 Cal. App.3d 814 (1976).

Restatement (Second) of Contracts § 4 (1981).

Ross v. Creighton University, 957 F.2d 410 (7th. Cir. 1992).

Sain v. Cedar Rapids Community School District, 626 N.W.2d 115 (2001).

Smith, A. A. (2016). Feds act against DeVry. Retrieved from https://www.inside highered.com/news/2016/01/28/ftc-and-education-department-take-action-against-devry-university

Stone, C. (2006). College advising and the courts. Retrieved from http://www.school counselor.org/magazine/blogs/may-june-2006/college-advising-and-the-courts

Stratford, M. (2015). Large for-profit settlements. Retrieved from https://www.insidehigh ered.com/news/2015/11/17/obama-administration-states-reach-major-settlements-education-management-corporation

Supplee v. Miller-Motte Business Colleg, 768 S.E.2d 582 (2015).

Taylor, A. N. (2015). Ending the higher education sucker sale toward an expanded theory of tort liability. *Utah L. Rev., 2015,* 425–478.

Tokic, S. (2014). Rethinking educational malpractice are educators rock stars? *B.Y.U. Educ. & L.J., 2014,* 105–133.

RHONDA VICKERS BEASSIE, *Assistant General Counsel, Texas State University System.*

8

An awareness of the relevant legal issues and an understanding of the appropriate times to engage legal counsel are essential skills for institutional research (IR) professionals.

The Value of Law in Assessment and Institutional Research

Gage Paine, JD, PhD

In 1819, the Supreme Court was asked to make a decision in what is usually referred to as the "Dartmouth College case" (*Trustees of Dartmouth College v. Woodward*, 1819). Starting with a reference to the 1769 document incorporating the Trustees of Dartmouth, this case is still taught today as the first clarification of the legal distinctions between public and private colleges (Olivas, 2006, p. 32). This was one of the first instances of the law resolving an issue in higher education, but it certainly was not the last. In other words, to wish for a return to some time in a mythical past when higher education was an ivory tower separate from the law is to misunderstand the many connections between the two areas of practice. To study the law of higher education is to study the history of education, and it becomes clear that many of our practices on campus today have been fashioned by the law in one way or another and that the interweaving of legal and educational practice began much earlier than most of us realize.

Where Does the Law Fit in Higher Education?

Education and law are quite distinct practices and have very different purposes. As the chapters in this monograph point out, for university administrators to do their jobs effectively, it is important to have a clear understanding of the ways education and law differ, the appropriate use of legal advice in educational decision making, and the most effective methods for achieving our educational goals without running afoul of the law. "Let's call the lawyers!" is rarely an educator's enthusiastic response when faced with a potential roadblock caused by institutional policies or legal questions. In fact, more often university administrators work to find ways to avoid involving campus legal counsel in matters of educational practice and decision making. On the whole, educators want to have open

New Directions for Institutional Research, no. 172 © 2017 Wiley Periodicals, Inc.
Published online in Wiley Online Library (wileyonlinelibrary.com) • DOI: 10.1002/ir.20207

and easy access to information, be able to engage in interesting and occasionally risky activities, and have the opportunity to push the boundaries of human knowledge in ways that have not been tried before. Educators are, by nature, innovators who want to create programs that haven't been tried before, collect and use data in new configurations, and share novel information with others—all of which most lawyers would classify as risky.

Lawyers, by training, are risk averse, or at least very calculating of risk. Clients who never do anything new and innovative create the least risk, while educators like those described above create and invite a great deal of risk, particularly if they avoid partnering with legal counsel in their pursuit of invention and discovery. Unfortunately, this perceived risk aversion is often the reason educators avoid contacting their lawyers; attorneys' tendencies to enumerate all of the factors that can go wrong or pitfalls to avoid are frequently seen as the equivalent of saying "don't do this." And the law, regulations, and even institutional policy are understood, at best, as a hindrance to the work of educators, deterrents promulgated by lawyers or administrators who do not understand education's fundamental purpose or, at worst, as restraints actually designed to stop people from doing creative, interesting, and necessary work.

Reframing the Law as a Starting Point

These perceptions—or misperceptions—result from the fundamental misunderstanding of the place of most laws and policies in decision-making processes. If law and policy are stopping educators from doing their best work, it means the law and lawyers are being consulted too late, or given the final veto. For example, faculty member A designs a new and interesting line of research regarding student alcohol use and its effect on graduation rates. To do the research, she defines the questions, delineates the information needed to answer those questions, and makes a request for the relevant student data including demographic information from the college or university; then someone tells her she cannot have the data. Her request runs into an institutional policy, a state regulation, a federal law, a staff member's interpretation of a policy or law, or all of the above. And, though there are usually processes to appeal these decisions or individuals she can lobby about her research, the goal has now become getting past the denial because the law, policy, or regulation is perceived to be the authority. This dynamic often makes finding a solution more difficult since it is harder to redesign or 'fix' a problem than it is to design a program that takes all of the appropriate policies and procedures into account at the start.

But there are other ways to handle—or avoid—such an outcome. What if we understand the law as the starting point rather than as a barrier to our creativity or the final step to getting approval? What if we understand law in its more appropriate place, as the least we have to do to stay out of trouble, the baseline from which we craft our plans and design our research? What if we understand it as the starting point to best practices? What if, instead of going to legal counsel at the end of our creative process, we instead sat down with legal counsel or a colleague who knows university policies and federal regulations, explained our goals, and asked, "How can I make this work?" This does not mean faculty member A has lost before she started; it is a reframing of the law as a foundation rather than a hurdle.

When we reframe the law as our first, instead of our last, step, when we understand laws and policies as a framework within which to operate instead of a barricade, we may be surprised by the opportunities for innovation. What if we work alongside our law and policy experts and ask, "How many ways can I achieve my purpose within the framework provided?" Instead of framing our questions as "Can I?" or "Why can't I?" what if we ask for help in achieving our goals? What if we were to understand our legal colleagues as partners rather than adversaries? As author, faculty member, and lawyer Peter Lake (Lake, 2011) frames the problem, "The hobgoblin of legal compliance is reductionism: that is, trying to reduce the law to a finite set of compliance solutions or one simple solution. In reality, legal compliance often requires the exercise of *judgment*—especially in higher education—and there is a range of possible compliance solutions. Often, there are no clear right or wrong answers at all—simply various choices with relative pros and cons. Indeed, it is the *process* of reaching decisions that is the most important" (p. 9).

Understanding Assessment and Institutional Research Questions Using the Lens of the Law

Let's look at a couple of examples of ways to frame and reframe the issues that assessment and institutional research leaders face.

Student Data and the Law.   In Chapter 3, Beaudin delineates some of the many laws related to data storage, the permissible and impermissible releases of student data, and the very real risks related to breaches in the security of such data. After reading the numerous requirements for and the issues surrounding the management of student data, an educator could understandably ask why a college or university would ever want to get into the student data business. But in many ways, student data storage is our lifeblood; a significant part of what we do is collect and certify to outside agencies what each of our students has studied, courses they have completed and the level of achievement they have attained—maintaining secure and accurate student transcripts is critical to the trust people place in higher education and the futures for which we are preparing our students. Transcript data, for example, are so important that when a campus closes, one of the critical issues to be managed is the transfer of that data to another equally qualified institution of higher education. The importance of that role is one of the reasons this area is so highly regulated yet also highly in demand.

NEW DIRECTIONS FOR INSTITUTIONAL RESEARCH • DOI: 10.1002/ir

The first question, whether or not we should store student data, is answered: Storing student data is a risk institutions of higher education must accept. The second question, "What are the laws and external regulations that govern the storage of student data?" will require the involvement of legal counsel. What is critical to understand here is that the answer to this question only defines the framework for decision making around student data; it does not define the decisions of what data to maintain or what policies are needed to determine who can access the data or the reasons for access. But the legal questions set the framework within which we can begin to ask the educational questions. For what educational purposes do we need to maintain data and for what purposes are data unnecessary? What data is needed to meet those educational purposes? How do we provide the widest access to make it possible for faculty and staff to design creative and innovative research activities and programs and services to educate and support students while simultaneously protecting the integrity and security of the data? What are the minimums and maximums here? Neither total access nor total restriction is appropriate, and zero risk is unrealistic and unattainable. This is the point of necessary tension between law and practice, which is when the exercise of judgment, as noted by Lake (2011, p. 9), comes into play. One cannot and should not look to law to solve all professional problems, especially given the complexities of modern higher education. At the same time, one cannot and should not ignore legal and regulatory realities because they seem inconvenient.

When all of the questions have been asked and all of the risks identified, when the appropriate educational decision-maker has a full understanding of the relevant parameters, then it is time for him or her to exercise judgment. The decision maker is rarely the lawyer. It is the responsibility of the assessment or institutional research administrator to make the best decision possible for the educational purposes of the institution within the defined framework. This is putting law and policy in its appropriate place within the educational mission of the institution.

Accreditation and the Law

Chapter 6 illustrates another of the challenges we face in understanding the law of higher education—as purposes change over time, so can the applicable legal questions. As Flood and Roberts point out, the change of the accreditation process, from a voluntary process created by professionals to support institutional improvement and maintain educational quality to a process of monitoring expectations set, indirectly, by the federal government, leads to a significant change in the relevant legal questions and applicable legal theories. Institutional research staff can legitimately be confused at the turns a process can take over the course of time.

The language of accreditation organizations is the language of collegial decision making and responsible self-governance. For example, the Middle

States Commission on Higher Education (MSCHE, 2016) defines itself as a "voluntary, non-governmental, regional membership association" and states that its accreditation process "ensures institutional accountability, self-appraisal, improvement, and innovation through peer review." The Southern Association of Colleges and Schools Commission on Colleges (SACSCOC, 2016) declares its mission is "to assure the educational quality and improve the effectiveness of its *member* institutions" (emphasis added). As an organization, SACSCOC is comprised of a college delegate assembly made up of one voting member from each accredited institution. They, in turn, elect members to the board of trustees. While there are staff members who do the day-to-day work of the accreditation process, the decisions regarding accreditation are made by representatives of the member organizations (SACSCOC, 2016). In other words, accreditation is an exercise in shared governance. All of that language, and more like it, describes a particular type of relationship between an accrediting agency and its member institutions—voluntary, collegial, collaborative—that would lead to one kind of legal analysis if disputes arise. In most cases that would be a reference back to the internal rules and agreements between the parties only.

But as Flood and Roberts explain, that relationship changed in the middle of the 20th century when the preexisting accreditation process was linked to access to federal dollars. On the face of it, this makes sense; an evaluation process already existed, so why should the government create a new, additional process? However, this link has fundamentally changed the nature of the relationship in ways that are easy to forget in the midst of all that has to be done to meet the needs of the accreditation process.

It's also important to understand that this relationship is still evolving, as the federal government has changed from a model of indirect lending to direct lending. Before 2010, the government "subsidized private lenders, who were the direct lenders to students and entrusted accrediting bodies with the power to determine which institutions would qualify for direct loans .... This longstanding system gave public regulation of higher education a very private feel. The federal government was not setting standards directly .... Even states that provided substantial support for higher education often deferred substantially to accrediting bodies" (Lake, 2011, pp. 73–74, citing U.S. Department of Education). The current preference for direct lending, as well as the changes in rules regarding qualification for financial aid designed to address abuses within some for-profit colleges, have led to, some speculate, more direct regulation of other institutions of higher education (Lake, 2011, p. 74).

The critical higher education accreditation process and its importance with regard to access to federal dollars make this a pertinent topic for discussion with campus counsel. External counsel may have no familiarity with this topic, and even in-house counsel may not understand the wide variety of issues and risks associated with the accreditation process. In such cases, the tendency for some attorneys may be to cite relevant law and

NEW DIRECTIONS FOR INSTITUTIONAL RESEARCH • DOI: 10.1002/ir

consider the matter closed. But it will be important for institutional research staff to help educate counsel on the other critical, nonlegal questions that need to be considered. For example, developing a new course of study for the campus calls into play the legal issues of academic freedom, but it also necessitates an understanding of campus practices regarding shared governance, responsibility for the curriculum, and the administrative practices of the accrediting body, to name just a few. Even developing policies and practices for certifying the qualifications of faculty to teach courses, as required by accrediting agencies, can involve a number of internal policies and practices and touch on a variety of legal issues, including employment law. Taking time to keep counsel up to date on changes in rules and potential risks, instead of acting as if the law has no place in the accreditation process, is valuable practice for the campus experts on accreditation.

Negligence, Access to Student Information, and the Law

Chapter 5 on negligence and the example of campus "early warning" systems as related to the development, maintenance, and use (or lack thereof) of data (knowledge) also illustrates this tension between law and educational practices. Letzring explicates the ways in which knowledge is legally known by the institution and details key considerations once someone is aware that something is amiss—that there are concerns about a student. The legal questions in this illustration arise when someone sees the need for an early warning system to catch students who are having trouble academically and begins to talk with people across campus about the idea. Some people catch on immediately and are ready to sign on, others are concerned about extra work and suggest finding out what data is already available. At some point, institutional research is brought into the discussion because of the data questions. The Family Educational Rights and Privacy Act (FERPA) provides guidelines for institutions, yet many questions arise in applying the law to the unique and complicated real life of students; this blanket set of rules is often hard to interpret when trying to help students struggling with myriad circumstances. These laws become even harder to interpret when students also battle with personal or social challenges. Even when staff identify FERPA as an issue, rarely, if ever, is legal counsel brought into such a discussion when the issues are primarily academic.

Change the scenario to behavioral concerns and the opposite is true. In these cases, the legal issues immediately arise and, in fact, help define the questions being asked. Behavioral assessment teams, by one name or another, have been created on campuses across the country to address crises after the shooting at Virginia Tech. These groups have been formed specifically to address behaviors that raise concerns, such as students behaving oddly in class, students saying strange things to roommates, students ending up being noticed by the police on multiple occasions, up to and including being referred to the conduct staff. In this situation, legal counsel is often involved from the beginning since the first questions asked are Who keeps the information? Is this information FERPA protected? and (at public institutions of higher education) Is it subject to open records requests? Additionally, for some students, issues can arise that are covered by the Americans with Disabilities Act (ADA), introducing another set of considerations. With that list of questions, legal counsel is often—and should always be—included in early meetings. The challenge in this circumstance is not whether to involve attorneys but how to give their counsel appropriate weight in the process.

The reality is that legal counsel should be involved in both kinds of discussions and needs to be consulted during policy development *and* when a problem needs to be solved. In both of these situations, it is possible that legal counsel will enumerate a long list of risks and issues. Depending on both the lawyer's approach and the administrator's experience with legal issues, that list can be perceived as anything from merely a list of items for consideration to a litany of disasters waiting to happen that will plunge the institution directly into a lawsuit. Regardless of the tone, it's important to understand the difference between a list of things that need to be taken into consideration and a list of actions that are truly against policy or law. Administrators need to learn to ask questions, press for a copy of the relevant law, or argue a different point of view. Lawyers are trained to be able to frame an argument in multiple ways and examine conflicting points of view; they should be engaged in the process of finding a solution to the legal issues connected to the educational questions being asked.

The fact that it is difficult to solve the very important and real legal questions asked with regard to record management is not a reason to dismiss the idea of creating behavior assessment teams. The potential notice issues are not a reason to stop an enterprising staff member from working to create an early warning system. Nor should legal questions or potential legal concerns stop the development of legitimate and important educational programs. The role of assessment and institutional research directors is to be cognizant of the relevant legal issues and risks and then apply that information as one consideration in deciding what programs and services should be developed or, if circumstances have changed, continued.

Conclusion

The fundamental educational values illustrated by the examples discussed throughout this monograph must not be set aside without compelling reasons. Even in situations where legal considerations and good educational practices seem to be in conflict, understanding the underlying purposes of both the law and the proposed program can help us find a way through to the best possible solution. Working to understand the applicable legal principles and then giving legal advice the appropriate weight in the current circumstances can help staff members create good practices and programs that meet institutional needs and do not run afoul of the law. Legal considerations do not necessarily contradict good educational practices; in fact, they should be understood as supporting good practice.

The chapters in this monograph cover a wide range of legal topics and issues related to the work of institutional research. Some are directly related to assessment and institutional research. Others are more connected with the administrative responsibilities carried by all faculty and staff. All of them are areas that should be understood and added into the mix of decision making on a daily basis. Having an awareness of the legal issues in institutional research will help institutional researchers be more effective at their jobs. Understanding when and how to ask legal counsel is one more skill to learn in furtherance of that work. To end with a quote that sums it up, "The message is simple: Use law and legislation to manage higher education environments, but be careful not to allow law and legislation to supplant good ... practice" (Lake, 2011, p. 11).

References

Lake, P. F. (2011). *Foundations of higher education law & policy: Basic legal rules, concepts, and principles for student affairs*. Washington, DC: National Association of Student Personnel Administrators.

Middle States Commission on Higher Education. (2016). Mission statement. Retrieved September 21, 2016, from http://www.msche.org/?Nav1=ABOUT&Nav2=MISSION

Olivas, M. A. (2006). *The law and higher education: Cases and materials on colleges in court* (3rd ed.). Durham, NC: Carolina Academic Press.

Southern Association of Colleges and Schools Commission on Colleges. (2016). *Commission organization*. Retrieved September 21, 2016, from http://www.sacscoc.org/commorg1.asp

Southern Association of Colleges and Schools Commission on Colleges. (2016). Mission statement. Retrieved September 21, 2016, from http://www.sacscoc.org/

Trustees of Dartmouth College v. Woodward (17 U.S. 1819).

U.S. Department of Education. (n.d.). Database of accredited postsecondary institutions and programs. Retrieved August 8, 2010, from http://www.ope.ed.gov/accreditation

GAGE PAINE, JD, PhD, *Senior Consultant, Keeling and Associates, LLC.*

INDEX

NEW DIRECTIONS FOR INSTITUTIONAL RESEARCH
ORDER FORM SUBSCRIPTION AND SINGLE ISSUES

DISCOUNTED BACK ISSUES:

Use this form to receive 20% off all back issues of *New Directions for Institutional Research*.
All single issues priced at **$23.20** (normally $29.00)

TITLE	ISSUE NO.	ISBN
_____	_____	_____
_____	_____	_____
_____	_____	_____

Call 1-800-835-6770 or see mailing instructions below. When calling, mention the promotional code JBNND to receive your discount. For a complete list of issues, please visit www.wiley.com/WileyCDA/WileyTitle/productCd-IR.html

SUBSCRIPTIONS: (1 YEAR, 4 ISSUES)

☐ New Order ☐ Renewal

U.S.	☐ Individual: $89	☐ Institutional: $362
CANADA/MEXICO	☐ Individual: $89	☐ Institutional: $404
ALL OTHERS	☐ Individual: $113	☐ Institutional: $440

Call 1-800-835-6770 or see mailing and pricing instructions below.
Online subscriptions are available at www.onlinelibrary.wiley.com

ORDER TOTALS:

Issue / Subscription Amount: $ _____

Shipping Amount: $ _____
(for single issues only – subscription prices include shipping)

Total Amount: $ _____

SHIPPING CHARGES:

First Item	$6.00
Each Add'l Item	$2.00

(No sales tax for U.S. subscriptions. Canadian residents, add GST for subscription orders. Individual rate subscriptions must be paid by personal check or credit card. Individual rate subscriptions may not be resold as library copies.)

BILLING & SHIPPING INFORMATION:

☐ **PAYMENT ENCLOSED:** *(U.S. check or money order only. All payments must be in U.S. dollars.)*

☐ **CREDIT CARD:** ☐ VISA ☐ MC ☐ AMEX

Card number _____ Exp. Date _____

Card Holder Name _____ Card Issue # _____

Signature _____ Day Phone _____

☐ **BILL ME:** *(U.S. institutional orders only. Purchase order required.)*

Purchase order # _____
Federal Tax ID 13559302 • GST 89102-8052

Name _____

Address _____

Phone _____ E-mail _____

Copy or detach page and send to: **John Wiley & Sons, Inc. / Jossey Bass**
PO Box 55381
Boston, MA 02205-9850

PROMO JBNND